Amy Barnes

Cooking School Recipes

Amy Barnes

Cooking School Recipes

ISBN/EAN: 9783744788748

Printed in Europe, USA, Canada, Australia, Japan

Cover: Foto ©Lupo / pixelio.de

More available books at **www.hansebooks.com**

COOKING SCHOOL RECIPES.

COMPILED BY

MISS BARNES,

FOR

Minneapolis and St. Paul Classes.

MINNEAPOLIS, MINN.
ALFRED ROPER, PRINTER, 305 HENNEPIN AVE.
1890.

"To be a good cook means the knowledge of all fruits, herbs, balms and spices; and of all that is healing and sweet in fields and groves, savory in meats. It means carefulness, inventiveness, watchfulness, willingness and readiness of appliance. It means the economy of your great grandmother and the science of modern chemists; it means much tasting and no wasting; it means English thoroughness, French art and Arabian hospitality; it means, in fine, that you are to be perfectly and always ladies, (loaf givers), and you are to see that everybody has something nice to eat."—*Ruskin.*

ABBREVIATIONS.

Tbsp. stands for Tablespoonful.　　m. stands for minute.
tsp.　" 　" teaspoonful.　　　　　　h.　" 　" hour.
ssp.　" 　" saltspoonful.　　　　　　qt.　" 　" quart.
c.　　" 　" cupful.　　　　　　　　　pt.　" 　" pint.

TABLE.

4 saltspoonfuls = 1 teaspoonful.
3 teaspoonfuls = 1 tablespoonful.
8 tablespoonfuls = 1 gill.
2 gills = 1 cup.
2 cups. = 1 pint.
2 pints. = 1 quart.

TABLE OF WEIGHTS AND MEASURES.

4 cupfuls of flour = 1 pound.
2　　"　　solid butter = 1 pound.
2　　"　　granulated sugar = 1 pound.
3　　"　　meal = 1 pound.
1 pint of milk or water = 1 pound.
1　　"　　chopped meat, packed tightly = 1 pound.
10 medium eggs, 9 large eggs = 1 pound.
1 round tablespoonful of butter = 1 ounce.
1 hp. tablespoonful of sugar = 1 ounce.
1 tablespoonful of liquid = ½ ounce.
1 small bottle of Burnett's Extra = 12 teaspoonfuls.
4 tablespoonfuls of liquid = 1 wineglass or ¼ cup.
1 speck = $\frac{1}{32}$ of teaspoonful or ⅛ saltspoonful.

INTRODUCTION.

Food is that which nourishes the body.

Cooking is the preparation of food by the aid of heat.

We *cook* our food to make it more digestable and more palatable.

Measuring.

The following rules are given as helps in measuering exactly:

The salt, teaspoon and tablespoons used in these recipes, are the size of the silver spoons now in general use. By reference to the table the relative size will be quickly seen. A spoonful of any kind of seasoning, spice, soda, cream of tartar, salt, etc., is measured by taking up a spoonful lightly, and leveling it with a knife. Flour, sugar, butter, meal, baking powder, etc., are measured rounding.

A rounding spoonful is measured by taking a spoonful of the material, and lightly shaking till the material is as convex on the top as the spoon is concave.

INTRODUCTION.

One-half a spoonful is one divided lengthwise of the spoon.

One-fourth, one-half of that, etc.

A speck is $\frac{1}{32}$ of a teaspoonful.

Cupfuls and fractions of cupfuls should always be measured exactly level.

Flour should be sifted *before* measuring.

Butter always packed down tightly in measuring.

A spoonful of *melted butter* is measured *after* melting.

A spoonful of *butter melted* is measured *before* melting.

The beaded tin-measuring cups make the measuring much easier and more exact.

MIXING.

There are three kinds of mixing—*stirring, beating* and *folding.*

We *stir* when we wish to *blend* two or more ingredients, as butter and sugar for cake; flour and milk in a batter, etc. To stir, keep the spoon in the mixture, resting the tip of the spoon on the bottom of the bowl, move the spoon in circles, and at the same time mash the mixture with the back of the spoon on the sides of the bowl.

We *beat* to entangle air in the mixture, as in eggs, or a batter. To beat a mixture, tip the bowl slightly, move the spoon in circles, so that the edge of the spoon scrapes the sides of the bowl; with a long, quick flop, bring the spoon up through the mixture into the air, and down again into the mixture on the opposite side.

We *fold* to *avoid* breaking the air cells, as when beaten whites of eggs or whipped cream are to be mixed with other material. To fold, turn the mixture over with the spoon, cut through, lifting the part from below up and over, fold gently, and *not stir* round and round.

Simmering is cooking in a liquid at the simmering point. That of water is 180°, F. Meats cooked in water, when the juice is desired *in* the meat, should be put into *boiling* water for a few minutes, this hardens the albumen on the entire surface, and forms a coating, through which the juice cannot escape. After this has been done, place the water where it will *simmer* till the meat is tender. Eggs should always be simmered, when cooked in water.

Boiling is cooking in a liquid at the boiling point. Water boils at 212°, F.; milk at 196°, F. Boiling water softens the woody fiber of vegetables, breaks the starch cells and cooks the starch. So we *boil* all vegetables and cereals when cooked in a liquid, and always cook them at a temperature equal to that of boiling water.

Baking is cooking by dry heat, as in an oven. The heat of the oven varies from a cool oven, which would be 150°, F., to a hot oven, which reaches 400°, F.

Here are a few simple tests for telling the heat of the oven.

Put a piece of white paper into the oven, and note the number of minutes it takes it to become colored.

For sponge cake, and pound cake, the paper should become light yellow in five minutes, for cup cake, the paper should become dark yellow, for bread and pastry, the paper should become dark brown.

Muffins made with eggs, and baking-powder, the paper should become dark brown in four minutes.

For water gems, and baking-powder biscuit, the paper should become dark brown in one minute.

When meat cannot be cooked directly exposed to the fire, as in a tin kitchen, or in a gas stove, which is true *roasting*, put it into a *hot* oven at first, then reduce the heat a little. Baste often, and have the ventilator of the oven open.

Broiling is cooking with the article directly exposed to a hot fire. The fire should be bright and clear, and, if a coal fire, the drafts should all be open. The success of broiling consists in *constant turning*. A general rule is to turn every ten seconds. A double broiler is the most convenient utensil for broiling.

Frying is cooking by immersion in hot fat.

INTRODUCTION.

Cottolene is the best fat for frying, next lard, or lard and drippings.

For potatoes or oysters, the fat should be hot enough to brown a small piece of bread the size of a croûton in 30 seconds, or at 400°, F.

For croquettes and all breaded articles, 380°, F or hot enough to brown the bread in 40 seconds.

For fritters, etc., 350°, F., or hot enough to brown the bread in 60 seconds.

Never use the fat unless fully heated. Drain all articles after frying on coarse brown paper.

Use a frying kettle and a basket for all small articles.

Avoid an accident when using fat by moving it always with caution, and being careful not to spill it on the stove. Strain always after using.

SOUPS.

Soups may be divided into two classes; those made with stock and those made without. As stock forms the foundation of many soups and sauces, the process of making should be thoroughly understood.

GENERAL DIRECTIONS FOR MAKING SOUP STOCK.

The meats used in making soup stock should contain gelatine, osmazome and fat.

Gelatine is found in bones, gristly portions of flesh and skin. It is not especially nutritious, has little flavor, but causes the stock to become a jelly when cold.

Osmazome gives to every kind of meat its distinctive flavor, and is found in the lean of beef, mutton, and fowls. We find more osmazome in the flesh of old animals than young, and most in the brown meats.

Fat should be used only in small quantities in soup stock. Much fat spoils the delicate flavors of the soup.

The marrow of the shin bone is the best fat to

use. The browned fat of roast beef gives a fine flavor, but mutton, ham and turkey fat should be avoided.

Cuts of meat for soup stock. Select a piece from shin, shank, or lower part of the round from beef or veal; from the fore-quarter and neck of mutton. Fowls are better than chickens.

Use any kind of cooked meat, one, or several kinds mixed, avoiding much ham. The greater the number of kinds used, the finer will be the flavor.

Remove any burnt or tainted portions, and the greater part of the fat.

Use a soup digester for making soup stock. This is a porcelain-lined, iron kettle, with a tight-fitting cover. If this is used, the liquor will evaporate but little and the fine flavor is retained.

The next best thing to a soup digester is a granite ware kettle with a tight-fitting cover.

To prepare the stock. If raw meat is used wipe it with a wet cloth; cut it into small pieces. Saw the bones into small pieces.

Put the fat in the bottom of the kettle, then the bones and the meat on top.

Add one quart of *cold* water to one pound of meat and bones, one and one-half pints of water, if wholly cooked meat is used.

Remember that cold water draws out the juice of the meat, while *hot* water hardens the albumen on the outside and *prevents* the juice from coming out.

Let the stock stand on the back of the range for an hour, to draw out the juices of the meat. When the water becomes quite red move the kettle toward the hotter part of the stove, and bring the water slowly to the boiling point. Then set it where it will *simmer* for six or eight hours.

Cooking at a high temperature will dissolve the lime in the bones and cloudy the soup. To extract the greatest amount of nutriment from the meat it must cook slowly and evenly.

> "A soup fast boiled
> Is a soup half spoiled."

Vegetables, herbs and spices, improve the stock. Use in the following proportions:

To every quart of water use one tablespoonful of carrot, turnip, celery and onion, a sprig of thyme, summer savory, sweet marjoram and parsley, one leaf sage and bay leaf, or one teaspooful of the mixed herbs, one small bit of celery root or saltspoonful celery seed, two peppercorns, two allspice berries, two whole cloves, one teaspoonful of salt.

Cut the vegetables, after washing and paring, into small cubes.

Use always the whole herbs and spices, *never* the ground.

To get a dark *brown, richly colored* stock, reserve a portion of the meat, dredge it with flour

SOUPS.

and brown in a portion of the fat or a little butter, before adding it to the water.

Frying the vegetables in the fat, till brown, *but not* black, improves the flavor of the stock.

A tablespoonful of *caramel* will improve the color, or use Madame Perrin's Pâte Française.

When the soup stock has cooked, strain through a fine strainer into an earthen bowl or jar.

Let it cool quickly, and it will keep longer.

In summer time it is best not to cook the vegetables with the stock as it will sour more quickly.

When the stock is cold there will be three portortions; the sediment at the bottom, then a clear jelly if there has been sufficient gelatine in the meat, and the fat on the top. Remove the fat carefully and use for drippings. The jelly is for clear soups and sauces. The sediment for brown soups and sauces, or vegetable soups.

To Clear Soups.

If for any reason the stock is not as clear as is desired, use for every four quarts of soup stock, the whites of two eggs. Beat the eggs and stir into the stock. Bring it slowly to a boil and then set it back *immediately* where it will only *simmer* for one half an hour.

Then strain through a napkin, or jelly-bag.

Great care should be used to prevent a rapid boiling, as it is impossible to clear a soup that has been made cloudy by rapid boiling at this time. Soup stock will keep a week or sometimes longer in winter; two or three days in summer.

Soup stock will keep longer when the fat remains over the top, excluding the air.

By scalding the stock every two or three days it can be kept for a much longer time.

To remove small particles of fat from a jelly stock, which would make it cloudy, pass a napkin wet in *hot* water, over the top. The heat will melt the fat, and the cloth quickly absorb it.

To remove fat from a soup when hot, pass strips of porous brown paper over the surface White stock is made from chicken or veal.

Thickening for Soups.

If a soup is desired thick, but clear, use arrow root, corn starch, or "Tapioca Exotique."

Of arrowroot use one tablespoonful mixed with one cupful of cold stock till smooth, then stir into one quart boiling stock and cook one half hour.

Use corn starch in the same way, but this will always give a little cloudiness to the soup.

Use one tablespoonful of "Tapioca Exotique" sprinkled into one quart boiling stock, for a clear gelatinous soup, and cook one half hour. In this the grains will always be perceptible, but it is very nice for a thick or clear soup.

For white and cream soups, rice, bread, barley,

SOUPS. 15

flour, corn starch, arrowroot, and "Tapioca Exotique" are used.

For a *brown* thick soup the flour is first browned in a dry pan, or browned with an equal volume of hot butter.

In either way the flour should be stirred constantly to prevent scorching.

The dry browned flour may always be kept on hand.

BOUILLON.

Clear beef from round, 5 lbs.
Cold water, 2 quarts.
Onion, 2 tablespoonfuls.
Turnip, 2   "
Celery, 2   "
Whites of Eggs, 2.
Peppercorns, 12.
Whole cloves, 4.

Cinnamon, 1 inch stick.
Salt, 1½ teaspoonfuls.
Parsley, 1 sprig.
Thyme, 1 sprig.
Summer Savory, 1 sprig.
Bay leaf, 1.
Sage leaf, 1.

Remove the fat from the meat, and cut the meat into small pieces. Reserve one fourth of the meat and put the remainder into the soup kettle with the cold water, let it stand on the back of the stove for an hour, then bring it *slowly* to a boil, and set it back where it will simmer for six hours. A slight bubbling on one side of the kettle will be sufficient.

At the end of that time add the vegetables, herbs and spices, and cook an hour longer. When this time has passed, strain, and set away to cool. In the morning remove the fat, and put the stock into the soup kettle, add the reserved raw beef, chopped very fine, and the whites of eggs beaten. Place on the stove and heat slowly, stirring occasionally. When it begins to boil, remove to a place where it will keep just below the boiling point for one hour, then add more salt and pepper, if needed and strain through a napkin.

Use one half box of gelatine soaked in one cupful of cold water, if more body is desired. Add with the whites of eggs.

Serve in soup plates if for dinner, or in cups if for luncheon or evening parties.

Consommé

Beef shank or lower part of round 4 lbs.
Shin of veal, 4 lbs.
Fowl, 5 lbs.
Cold water, 6 quarts.
Onion, 1 large.
Chopped carrots, 4 tablespoonfuls
Chopped Turnip, 4 "
Chopped celery, 4 "
Salt, 2 "
Butter, 4 "

Parsley, 1 sprig.
Thyme, 2 sprigs.
Summer savory, 2 sprigs.
Bay leaves, 3.
Sage leaves, 2.
Peppercorns, 40.
Cloves, 6.
Cinnamon, 3 inch sticks.
Mace, 1 blade.
Allspice berries, 10.
Whites of Eggs, 2.

Wipe the meat and cut into small pieces, reserving one-fourth of the beef. Saw the bones into small pieces.

Put a small quantity of the fat into the soup kettle, and then the bones, and the meat on top. Add the water, and let the kettle stand on the back of the stove for one hour. Wash and pare the vegetables and cut into small cubes, fry in the butter till light brown, then add to the stock. Dredge the reserved beef with flour and brown it in the remaining butter, and then add to the stock. Simmer two hours then add the fowl, which has been cleaned thoroughly. Simmer till the fowl is tender, then remove it. It will have imparted a good flavor to the stock. When the stock has simmered six or eight hours, strain through a fine strainer, and put it where it will cool quickly. In the morning it will be a jelly. Remove every particle of fat, put the jelly into a sauce pan, add the whites of eggs, beaten light, heat slowly to the boiling point, then keep it just below that for one half an hour. Then it should be clear, with the whites of eggs cooked in one dry stiff mass. Add salt and pepper if needed. Strain through a napkin. Serve clear, or it may be garnished.

Consommé with Macaroni.

Consomme, 1 quart.
Macaroni, 3 sticks.
Salt, 1 teaspoonful.
Boiling water, 1 quart.

Boil the maccaroni in the water with the salt for half an hour. Then drain, and pour several quarts of cold water over it. Place on a board, and cut into one inch to one-eighth inch pieces. Bring the consommé to a boil, add the maccaroni, and when hot, serve. Vermicelli, rice, barley, and French paste may be used in the same way. Use one tablespoonful of rice or barley to one quart of stock. Boil rice half hour; vermicelli, or French paste, ten minutes; barley, five hours.

Consommé with Green Peas.

Consomme, 3 pints.
Fresh green peas, or
French canned peas, 1 cupful.

Boiling water, 2 quarts.
Salt, 1 teaspoonful.

Boil the fresh peas in the water with the salt for twenty minutes, or till tender, drain and add to the consommé. Boil gently five minutes. If French peas are used drain, and pour cold water over them, then proceed as for fresh peas.

Consommé with Asparagus.

Asparagus tops, ½ pint.
Consomme, 1 quart.

Boiling water, 1 quart.
Salt, 1 teaspoonful.

Use the delicate asparagus tops, and boil in the water with the salt for fifteen minutes. Drain, and put into a sauce pan with the consommé. Boil gently five minutes and serve.

Consommé à la Royale.

Consomme, 1 quart.
Eggs, 2.

Salt, ¼ teaspoonful.
Milk, 2 tablespoonfuls.

Beat the eggs till smooth, add salt and milk. Turn into a buttered cup. Set the cup into a pan of warm water, and bake in a slow oven. When a

SOUPS.

knife, put down through the center will come out dry, it is done. Set away to cool. When cold, cut into thin slices and then cut into pretty shapes with vegetable cutters. Put them into the soup tureen and pour the hot soup over it.

JULIENNE SOUP.

Clear stock, 2 quarts.
Turnips, carrots and celery, mixed 1 pint.
Lettuce, finely shredded, 1 pint.
Sorrel ½ cupful.

Cut the vegetables into fine strips, one inch long. Shred the lettuce and sorrel very fine. Cook the vegetables in boiling, salted water till tender, and drain. It will take one half hour. Put the lettuce with one cupful of boiling water into a sauce pan, boil ten minutes, and drain. Wash the sorrel and cover with cold water. Bring the stock to a boil, add vegetables, lettuce and sorrel, and more salt and pepper if needed, boil gently fifteen minutes and serve.

Other kinds of vegetables may be substituted in varying quantities, green peas, cauliflower, onions, etc.

SCOTCH BROTH.

Neck of mutton, 2 lbs.
Carrots, turnips, onions and celery, mixed, 1 cupful.
Chopped parsley, 1 tablespoonful.
Pearl barley, 1 cupful.
Cold water, 2 quarts.
Flour, 1 tablespoonful.
Butter, 1   "
Salt, 2 teaspoonfuls.
Pepper, 2 saltspoonfuls.

Cut the meat into small pieces and remove the

fat. Cut the vegetables into one-fourth inch cubes. Chop the parsley fine. Soak the barley over night. Put the meat into a sauce pan, add vegetables, barley, three pints of water, salt and pepper. Put the bones into another sauce pan and add one pint of water. Simmer both mixtures three hours. Then cook the butter and flour together till smooth and frothy, add some of the soup till thin enough to pour, then turn into the soup, add the liquor in which the bones were cooked, and the parsley, and serve.

The success of this soup depends upon the long, slow cooking, and upon the vegetables and meat being in *small* pieces. Then it is very nice.

Imperial Soup.

Chicken Stock, 1 quart.	Butter, 2 tablespoonfuls.
Cream, 1 pint.	Salt, 1½ teaspoonfuls.
Stale bread, ½ pint.	Pepper, 1 saltspoonful.
Breast of fowl, ½.	Clove, 1.
Yolks of eggs, 4.	Parsley, 1 sprig.
Carrot, 1 tablespoonful.	Thyme, 1 sprig.
Onion, 1 "	Cinnamon, 1 inch stick.
Celery, 1 "	Mace, 1 blade.
Flour, 1 "	

Clean a fowl and cover with three quarts cold water. Simmer two or three hours, till tender. Remove the fowl and reduce the stock to three pints. Strain and set away to cool. When cold, remove the fat, put the quart of stock into a sauce pan with the bread free from crust. Simmer one hour. Put the vegetables, cut fine, with the butter, into a frying pan, cook slowly twenty minutes, being careful not to burn them. Then skim out the vegetables and put them into a muslin bag with the herbs and spice. This is to keep them from coloring the soup. Cook with the stock for the remainder of the hour.

Add the flour to the butter remaining in the pan, cook till smooth and frothy, and then add to the soup. Add the salt and pepper. Then chop the breast of the fowl very fine and then pound to a powder. At the end of the hour remove the bag of vegetables from the soup, put in the powdered chicken, add one a half cupfuls of the cream, and when hot strain through a puree strainer, then a French fine sieve.

Return to the fire in a double boiler. Beat the yolks of the eggs, add the remaining one half cupful of cream, and when the soup is hot, turn it in, stirring as you do so. Cook one minute, or till the egg stiffens. Add more salt and pepper if needed, and serve.

White Soup.

Chicken or veal stock, 1 quart.
Rice, 2 tablespoonfuls.
Celery, 2 stalks.
Blade of mace, 1.
Stick cinnamon, 1 inch.
Peppercorns, 6.
Onion, 1 tablespoonful.

Corn starch, 1 tablespoonful.
Butter, 1 "
Cream, 1 pint, or
Milk and cream, 1 pint.
Hard cooked eggs, 2.
Salt, 1½ teaspoonfuls.
Pepper, 1 saltspoonful.

Wash the rice through three waters. Put it in a sauce pan with the stock, add the celery, onion, spice, salt and pepper. Boil slowly till the rice has become very soft, one hour or more. Then cook the butter and corn starch together till smooth and frothy, and add to the soup. Scald the cream and add that. Strain through a fine french sieve, and return to the stove in the double boiler. When hot turn into the tureen and add the yolks of the eggs mashed through a fine sieve.

PUREE OF SALMON.

Salmon, ½ of a lb. can.
Milk, 1 quart.
Onion, ¼.
Butter, 1 tablespoonful.
Flour, 1 "

Salt, 1½ teaspoonfuls.
Pepper, 4 saltspoonful.
Parsley, 1 sprig.
Cayenne pepper, ¼ saltspoonful.

Remove all bones and skin from the salmon and chop it fine. Cook the milk, parsley and onion ten minutes in the double boiler. Then cook the butter and flour together till smooth and frothy, and add to it a little at a time the milk from the double boiler. Return all to the double boiler, add the salmon and seasoning, cook five minutes, and strain through a puree strainer.

CREAM OF COD SOUP.

Make like the preceding recipe, only substitute one cup of cooked cod, or any white fish, finely flaked.

SOUPS.

GREEN TURTLE SOUP

Green turtle, 1 can.
Water, 1 quart.
Peppercorns, 12.
Whole Cloves, 6.
Parsley, 2 sprigs.
Summer savory, 2 sprigs.
Salt, 1 teaspoonful.
Pepper, 1 saltspoonful.
Lemon, 1 tablespoonful.
Sweet marjoram, 2 sprigs.

Thyme, 2 sprigs.
Bay leaves, 2.
Sage leaves, 2.
Onion, 1.
Carrot, 1 tablespoonful.
Turnip, 1 "
Celery, 1 stalk.
Butter, 2 tablespoonfuls.
Flour, 2 "

The green turtle is boiled and put up in cans, for making soup. This is the best thing to use for those having small families.

Remove the fat from the meat and cut it into small cubes.

Add the water to the turtle and the whole spices. Fry the vegetables, cut in small cubes, in the butter, fifteen minutes. Then skim out the vegetables and add to the soup. Add the flour to the butter remaining in the pan, and cook till brown, then the soup till thin, and return to sauce pan with the meat, add salt and pepper, and simmer one hour. At the end of that time, strain. Cut the lemon into very thin slices. Put them into the soup tureen and pour the soup over them.

MOCK BISQUE SOUP.

Milk, 1 quart.
Tomatoes, 1 pint.
Onion, ½.
Butter, ⅛ cupful.

Corn starch, 1 tablespoonful.
Salt, 1 teaspoonful.
Pepper, ½ saltspoonful.
Soda, 1 "

Cook the onions with the tomatoes, ten minutes, and strain. Scald the milk. Cook the starch with one tablespoonful of the butter till smooth and frothy and then add the milk, gradually.

Return to the double boiler and add the seasoning. Just before serving, if the tomatoes are rather acid, add the soda, and then add the tomatoes to the thickened milk, strain and serve, with croûtons or crisped crackers.

Tomato Soup.

Tomatoes, 1 quart.
Boiling water, 1 pint.
Flour, 2 tablespoonfuls.
Butter, 2 "
Peppercorns, 2.

Whole Cloves, 2.
Salt, 1 teaspoonful.
Sugar, ½ teaspoonful.
Onion, ½.
Parsley, 1 sprig.

Boil the tomatoes, water, and seasoning for ten minutes. Then cook the butter and flour together till smooth and frothy, add the soup gradually. Mash through a fine sieve, all but the seasoning and vegetables. Serve with croûtons or crisped crackers.

Corn Soup.

Can of Corn, 1.
Milk, 1¼ quarts.
Buttter, 3 tablespoonfuls.
Flour, 2 "

Salt, 1½ teaspoonfuls.
Pepper, 1 saltspoonful.
Onion, 1 tablespoonful.
Yolks of Eggs, 2.

Mash the corn in a chopping tray, then put it into the double boiler with one quart milk, and cook fifteen minutes. Fry the onion in the butter for ten minutes, or till bright yellow. Add the flour, and cook till smooth and frothy, then add some of the soup gradually, till thin enough to pour, then return all to the double boiler, and add the salt and pepper and cook ten minutes longer. Strain through a fine puree strainer. Returned to the double boiler, beat the yolks of the eggs, add the remaining one cup of milk, and add to the soup. Cook till the egg stiffens, about five minutes, and serve.

If fresh corn is used, cut each ear of corn, and then scrape, thus removing the pulp and leave the hull on the cobb. Boil the cobbs ten minutes in one pint of water, and use this in place of one pint of milk. There should be corn pulp enough to make one pint. Old corn is better than young, which has only a milky juice.

GREEN PEA SOUP.

Fresh Peas, 1 quart, or
Canned " 1 can.
Stock or water, 1 pint.
Milk, 1 cup.
Cream, 1 cup.

Salt, 1 teaspoonful.
Pepper, 1 saltspoonful.
Butter, 1 tablespoonful.
Flour, 1 tablespoonful.
Onion, 1 small.

When fresh peas are used, put them in one pint boiling water, and boil with the onion till they will mash easily. Then add the one pint of stock or water.

If canned peas are used, add this at first and

cook till they will mash easily. When soft, cook the butter and flour together till smooth and frothy, add the soup to it gradually, and return to the saucepan. Add the milk, cream, salt and pepper. Strain through a fine puree strainer, mashing all the pulp through. Heat again, being careful not to burn it, and serve. Old, hard peas may be used, but must be cooked till soft. A cupful of whipped cream added after the soup goes into the tureen is a pleasing addition.

Potato Soup.

Potatoes, 6.
Milk, 1 quart.
Celery, 1 stalk.
Onion, 1 small.
Butter, 1 tablespoonful.

Flour, ½ tablespoonful.
Salt, 1 teaspoonful.
Pepper, 1 saltspoonful.
Celery salt, ½ teaspoonful.

Wash, pare and soak the potatoes in cold water ½ hour or longer time, if they are old. Cover them with boiling water and boil thirty minutes. Drain off all the water. In the meantime cook the milk, celery and onion in the double boiler ten minutes. Mash the potatoes till fine and light, then add the milk *gradually*, stirring all the while.

Strain through a fine sieve. Return to the double boiler. Cook the butter and flour together till smooth and frothy, and add the soup gradually. Then add the seasoning, and if you like, one teaspoonful chopped parsley.

FISH.

Swedish White Fish.

Fish, 2 or 3 lbs.
Milk, 1 pint.
Crackers, 3.
Eggs, 2.
Butter, 3 tablespoonfuls.

Sugar, 1 teaspoonful.
Salt, 1 saltspoonful.
Nutmeg, 1 "
Pepper, 1 "

Use cod, haddock, white fish or halibut.

Beat the eggs and add to them the milk, seasoning, and the crackers, broken into small pieces. While the crackers are soaking, clean, skin and bone the fish. Butter a tin sheet with one tablespoonful of the butter, and put it into the dripping pan. Lay one of the pieces of fish on it. Sprinkle with salt and pepper. Then add some of the crackers and custard. Cover with the remaining piece of fish, sprinkle with salt and pepper. Pour the remainder of the custard and crackers over the top. Add the second spoonful of butter. Bake fortyfive minutes. As soon as the custard stiffens, take it from the bottom of the pan and pour it over the fish. And so continue till *all* is on the fish. Then put the third spoonful of butter over the top and baste with it till the whole is golden brown. Serve with Hollandaise sauce, garnish with parsley.

Haddock Stuffed with Oysters.

Fish, 2 or 3 lbs.
Oysters, 1 pint.
Melted butter, ½ cup.
Eggs, 1.

Bread crumbs. ½ cup.
Cracker crumbs, ½ cup.
Salt, 1 teaspoonful.
Pepper, 1 saltspoonful.

Haddock, cod, halibut or white fish may be used for this dish.

Clean, skin and bone the fish. Butter a tin sheet, and place one half the fish upon it. Sprinkle with salt and pepper. Wash the oysters in their own liquor, free from shells, and drain. Dip the oysters into the butter and then roll in the cracker crumbs. Cover the fish with them, and lay the remaining piece of fish on top. Sprinkle with salt and pepper, brush with egg. Moisten the bread crumbs with the remainder of the butter and spread over the top. Fasten the fish in place with small wooden skewers (tooth picks will do). Bake from thirty to forty-five minutes, or till the fish is so tender that a skewer will pierce it easily. Serve with Hollandaise sauce and garnish with parsley.

Escaloped Fish.

Fish, 1 quart.
Milk, 1 pint.
Butter, 2 tablespoonfuls.
Flour, 2   "
Salt, 2 teaspoonfuls.

Pepper, ½ teaspoonful.
Onion, ½.
Parsley, 1 sprig.
Bread crumbs, ½ cup.
Butter, 1 tablespoonful.

FISH.

Put the fish in boiling water with one tablespoonful of salt. Simmer twenty minutes. Take up and drain. Remove skin and bones and measure about one quart of it. Flake it quite fine with a fork. Cook the milk with the onion and parsley ten minutes. Cook the butter and flour till smooth and frothy, then gradually add the milk. Remove the onion and parsley. Put one teaspoonful of salt and one saltspoonful pepper into the sauce and mix remainder with the fish. Butter an escaloped dish and put in a layer of sauce, then a layer of fish, and so continue till the dish is full. Melt one spoonful of butter, add the crumbs, and put over the top. Bake fifteen or twenty minutes.

Dropped Fish Balls.

Salt fish, 1 pint.
Pared potatoes, 1 quart.
Butter, 1 tablespoonful.

Eggs, 2.
Pepper, 1 saltspoonful.
Salt, if needed.

Wash, pare and soak the potatoes as for boiled potatoes. Shred the fish. Put the potatoes into a sauce pan, with the fish on top. Cover with boiling water. Boil 30 minutes, or till the potatoes are tender, then drain till fully dry and shake on the stove till floury. Mash, and add the butter, salt, pepper and the egg well beaten. Beat till smooth and light. To fry them, dip a tablespoon into the kettle of hot fat, take a spoonful of the mixture, smooth it with a knife, and then slide it into the fat. It should brown in two minutes. Drain on brown paper.

CREAMED OYSTERS.

Oysters, 1 quart.
Cream, 1 pint.
Butter, 1 tablespoonful.
Flour, 1 "

Salt, 1 teaspoonful.
Pepper, 1 saltspoonful.
Onion, ¼.
Mace, 1 blade.

Put the cream into the double boiler, and cook with the piece of onion and mace ten minutes. Cook the butter and flour in the frying pan till smooth and frothy, and then gradually add the cream. Remove the onion and mace, and add the salt and pepper. Wash the oysters, and cook in their liquor till they look plump and begin to curl. Then drain them and put into the sauce.

Serve in patties, or on toast, or in a potato border.

FRICASSEE OF OYSTERS.

Oysters, 1 pint.
Cream, ½ cup.
Oyster liquor, ½ cup.
Eggs, 1.
Butter, 2 tablespoonfuls.

Flour, 1 tablespoonful.
Lemon juice, 1 teaspoonful.
Pepper, ½ saltspoonful.
Salt, ½ teaspoonful.

Put one tablespoonful of butter into a frying pan, and when hot, put in the oysters, washed and drained. Cook till plump and drain again. Put the oyster liquor into a cup, and fill the cup with cream. Cook the flour with the remaining spoonful of butter till smooth and frothy, and add the liquor a little at a time. Then add the seasoning, and the egg beaten light, then the oysters, and as soon as hot, serve. Serve in bread or paste patties if for lunch or dinner; on toast for breakfast or tea.

MEATS, ENTREES AND RÉCHAUFFÉS.

Fillet of Beef, Larded.

The true fillet is the tenderloin. A short fillet weighing two and a half or three pounds willl be sufficient for ten persons, at a dinner, where this is served as one course.

Remove from the fillet all the muscle, ligament fat, and smooth tough covering. If not in good shape, skewer it into shape with small steel or wooden skewers.

Have some firm, solid, clear, fat, salt pork. Cut this into slices one-eighth inch thick, and cut this into three and a half inch strips, fit these lardoons into the larding needle and lard the fillet, putting two or three rows of lardoons on the top, lengthwise of the fillet. To lard, put the lardoon into the needle as far as it will go, and thrust the needle into the meat, taking a stitch, as it were, an inch long and $\frac{1}{4}$ inch deep in the meat ; leave the lardoon sticking out of the meat half an inch at each end. Have the lardoons in the two rows alternating.

MEATS, ETC.

The lardoon will slip from the needle as it leaves the meat.

Dredge the fillet with salt, pepper and flour, put it into a small pan, with some scraps of pork in the bottom, and cook in a hot oven thirty minutes. Baste often, and as soon as the flour is brown, with the fat in the pan. Serve with brown mushroom or tomato sauce.

Leg of Mutton, Stuffed and Roasted.

Use either a "raised shoulder" from the fore-quarter, or a leg of mutton. Remove the bone, keeping the meat as whole as possible. Wipe till clean with a wet cloth, stuff, and sew up securely into good shape. Sprinkle with salt, pepper and flour. Bake in a hot oven or roast for one hour, if wished rare; one and a half hours if wished well done. Baste often, and as soon as the flour browns. When half done turn the meat, and dredge with salt, pepper and flour.

Stuffing.

Mix one cup cracker or stale bread crumbs with one saltspoonful salt, thyme and pepper, one tablespoonful of chopped parsley, one tablespoonful of chopped onion, with one quarter cup of melted butter. If a moist stuffing is desired, add hot water till the crumbs hold together.

MEATS, ETC.

BEEF ROULETTE.

Round of beef, 2 or 3 pounds.
Chopped cooked ham, 1 cup.
Eggs, 1.
Mustard, 1 saltspoonful.
Cayenne pepper, 1 speck.
Salt Pork, or ham drippings, 4 tablespoonfuls.

Onions, chopped, 1.
Flour, 2 tablespoonfuls.
Boiling water, 1½ pints.
Whole Cloves, 2.
Salt, 1 teaspoonful.
Pepper, ¼ teaspoonful.

Have the beef cut *very* thin from the top of the round. Mix the ham, mustard, cayenne pepper and eggs together. Spread on the beef, roll up and tie securely. Dredge with salt, pepper and flour, and brown in the hot drippings. Remove to a small sauce-pan. Fry the onions five minutes in the fat remaining in the pan; then add the flour and cook till brown; then add the water gradually, boil up once, and pour over the roulette. Add the remainder of the seasoning and simmer three hours. Take up the roulette, remove the string and strain the gravy over it.

HAMBURG STEAKS.

Chop one pound of lean beef very fine, add to it one tablespoonful of onion juice, half teaspoonful of salt, quarter teaspoonful pepper, and mix well together.

Moisten the hands in cold water, take about one tablespoonful of the mixture, and shape into balls or small steaks. Put two tablespoonfuls of butter into a frying-pan, and when hot put in the steaks, brown on one side, then turn and brown on the other. Take up the steaks, and add to the butter remaining in the pan one teaspoonful of flour, when smooth and brown, add half pint of boiling water. Season with salt and pepper, and Worcestershire sauce or lemon juice. Strain over the steaks and serve. The steaks may be made in the same way, and broiled like plain steak, seasoned with salt, pepper, and spread with butter. Broil four minutes.

Broiled Beef Steak.

Cut the steak one inch thick. Wipe ; trim off superfluous fat and remove the bone. Sprinkle lightly with salt and pepper. Broil over a bright fire from four to ten minutes, turning every ten seconds. Remove to a hot platter, season with butter, salt and pepper, or serve with Maître d' Hôtel butter.

Broiled Chops en Papellote.

Wipe, trim, and sprinkle with salt and pepper, and wrap in buttered papers, turning up the edges like a turnover. Broil from eight to ten minutes. Remove the paper, place on a hot platter, cover the bone with paper ruffles, and garnish with parsely.

Pan-broiled Chops.

Wipe and trim the chops. Heat a frying pan *very* hot—till it smokes. Put in the chops, and turn every ten seconds; pour out every drop of fat as it comes from the chops, keeping the pan dry and very hot. Broil five minutes. In this way very fat chops may be browned without burning. Remove to a hot platter, and sprinkle with salt and pepper.

Mutton Chops, Breaded.

Wipe and trim, and sprinkle with salt and pepper. Dip in beaten egg, and then in sifted bread crumbs, drop into hot fat that will brown a piece of bread in forty seconds. When the crumbs are brown, remove the kettle to a cooler part of the stove. Fry eight minutes. Serve with tomato sauce, green peas, or mashed potatoes. Cover the bone with paper ruffles.

Veal Cutlets.

Slice of veal, 1.
Salt pork, ½ pound.
Stock or water, 1 pint.
Eggs, 1.
Bread Crumbs, 1 cup.

Salt, 1 saltspoonful.
Pepper, ½ saltspoonful.
Flour, 1 tablespoonful.
Lemons, 1.

One slice of veal from the leg. Wipe and remove the bone, skin and gristle. Cut into pieces the size of a mutton chop. Sprinkle with salt and pepper, dip in beaten egg, and then in the bread crumbs. Cut the pork into small pieces, and fry. Then fry the cutlets in the fat till brown on both sides. Then put the cutlets in a sauce-pan with the pork scraps. To the fat remaining in the pan —there should be two tablespoonfuls—add the flour, and brown it ; then add the stock or water, let it boil up, then add seasoning, and pour over the cutlets, and simmer forty-five minutes, or till the cutlets are tender. Remove to a platter, and strain the gravy over them. Use one tablespoonful of lemon juice in the gravy, and cut the remainder into thin slices and use as a garnish. Tomato catsup, Worcestershire sauce, or horseradish, may be used in place of the lemon, to season the gravy.

Casserole of Rice and Meat.

Rice, 1 cup.
Cold meat chopped, 1½ cups.
Salt, ¾ teaspoonful.
Pepper, 1 saltspoonful.
Celery salt, 1 "
Chopped onion, 1 teaspoonful.

Chopped parsley, 1 teaspoonful.
Thyme, 1 saltspoonful,
Sweet marjoram, 1 slatspoonful.
Cracker crumbs, 2 tablespoonfuls.
Eggs, 1.

Boil the rice till tender and drain. Butter a three-pint mould and sprinkle with fine bread crumbs. Line the bottom and sides one-half inch deep, with the rice. Mix the meat with the cracker crumbs, egg and seasoning, and moisten with hot water or stock, till as thin as a drop batter. Place this in the center of the mould, and cover with the remainder of the rice. Bake thirty minutes, or steam forty-five minutes. Turn it out, and pour tomato sauce over and around it.

RAGOUT OF MUTTON.

Cold meat, 1 quart.	Butter, 2 tablespoonfuls,
Onions, 12 button or 2 common.	Flour, 2 "
Carrots, 1.	Stock or water, 1 quart.
Turnip, 1.	Salt, 1 teaspoonful.
Potatoes, 3.	Pepper, 1 saltspoonful.

Cut the meat into inch cubes or thin slices, removing the greater part of the fat, and the gristle. Cut the vegetables into one-half inch cubes, or the potatoes may be cut larger, or into balls with a cutter. Cook the onions, carrot and turnip in salted boiling water till tender, and drain, The time will depend upon the age, varying from one-half hour to one and a half hours. The older the vegetables the longer it will take. Cook the butter and flour together till smooth and brown, then add the stock or water, slowly, then put in the meat and *simmer* till very tender. The time will depend on the kind of meat, varying from one-half to one hour. When tender add the vegetables, and cook fifteen minutes. Boil the potatoes in salted water ten minutes, or till tender, drain and add to the ragout just before serving. Season, and serve with a border of mashed potatoes, boiled rice or macaroni. Serve the meat in the center and the vegetables around it. Mutton, veal or beef may be used. If meat and vegetables are cooked till very tender and the ragout is well seasoned, it is very nice.

CURRY OF MUTTON.

Cold mutton, 1 pint.	Curry powder, 1 tablespoonful.
Butter, 1 tablespoonful.	Salt, 1 teaspoonful.
Onion, 1.	Stock or water, 1 pint.
Flour, 1 tablespoonful.	

Cut the meat into inch cubes, or slices. Fry the onion in the butter till yellow and then add the flour, curry powder and salt.. Cook till brown and then add the stock gradually. Put in the meat and simmer till tender. Serve with a border of boiled rice, or Turkish pilaf. A veal curry may be made in the same way. Raw meat may be used, but should be cooked a longer time.

BLANQUETTE OF CHICKEN.

Cold cooked chicken, 1 quart.	Nutmeg, 1 speck.
Chicken stock, 1 cup,	Pepper, 1 saltspoonful.
Cream, 1 cup.	Salt, 1 tablespoonfuls.
Butter, 2 tablespoonfuls.	Lemon juice, 1 tablespoonful.
Flour, 2 "	Yolks of eggs, 2.

Cut the chicken in one-half inch cubes.

Cook the butter and flour together till smooth and frothy, then add the chicken stock, a little at a time, and when that boils up add the cream, reserving one-fourth cupful. When hot, add the chicken and seasoning and cook ten minutes. Then beat the eggs and add to them the cold cream. At the end of the ten minutes, add the eggs, and cook till stiffened, which will be in five minutes. Taste, to see if more seasoning is needed, and serve in a potato or rice border, or on toast, and garnish with points of toast.

CHICKEN CHARTREUSE.

Cold cooked chicken, 9 ounces.
Lean cooked ham, 3 "
Sausages, 2.
Bread Crumbs, fine, 3 tablespoonfuls.
Capers, 1 tablespooful.
Lemon juice, 2 tablespoonfuls.
Cayenne pepper, speck.
Eggs, 2.

Chop the chicken and ham very fine add the inside of the sausages, crumbs, eggs beaten, and the seasoning. Mix well, add more salt and pepper if needed. The amount will depend upon the ham and sausages. Add enough hot stock to make as thin as a drop batter. Butter a quart mould, pack in the mixture tightly, cover with buttered paper, and steam three hours.

Serve as it is when cold, garnished with parsley, capers, and hard cooked eggs, or mould in jelly.

To mould in aspic Jelly.

Put one quart chicken stock, one-half teaspoonful of salt, one saltspoonful of celery salt, a bouquet of sweet herbs, the juice and rind of one-half a lemon, with the white of one egg beaten, with one-half box of gelatine which has been soaked in one-half cupful of cold water, into a saucepan. Bring the mixture slowly to a boil, and when a thick scum has formed, set it toward the back part of the stove for one-half hour. Strain through a napkin. Put a layer one-half inch deep into a three-pint mould. When this is stiff garnish with French paste, capers or vegetables, cut into fancy shapes.

Now put a few drops of the liquid jelly onto these to hold them in place. When this is stiff, remove the chicken from the mould and place carefully on the center of the jelly.

Pour the remainder of the jelly around the chicken, filling the space between the mould and the sides of the larger mould. Set away till the jelly is stiff. To turn out the chartreuse, wet the sides and bottom of the mould with warm water till a small amount of jelly is melted. Place a platter over the top of the mould, and then invert both quickly. Garnish with more of the aspic jelly cut into cubes, slices of lemon and parsley.

Chicken Croquettes.

Cooked chicken, 1 pint.
Milk or chicken stock, 1 pint.
Flour, 3 tablespoonfuls.
Butter, 3   "
Lemon juice, 3 tablespoonfuls.
Salt, 1½ teaspoonfuls.
Celery salt, ¾ teaspoonful.

Mace, 1 saltspoonful.
Onion juice, 1½ teaspoonful.
Chopped parsley, 1 tablespoonful.
Cayenne pepper, 1 speck.
Eggs, 2.
Bread crumbs, 1 pint.

Remove bone, skin and gristle and chop the chicken very fine. Scald the milk. Cook the butter and flour together till smooth and frothy, then add the milk, gradually, making a stiff white sauce. Add the sauce to the chicken, making the mixture a little thinner than can be handled. It will be stiffer when cold, and the softer the mixture, the more creamy will be the croquettes. Then add the seasoning, and mix *thoroughly*. Spread on a platter, and set away till cold. Beat the eggs on a plate till smooth. Sprinkle the sifted crumbs onto a bread board. Then take a heaping teaspoonful of the mixture, and make it into a ball, smoothing out all cracks or folds in the mixture. Then roll in the crumbs, pressing the ball till cylindrical, then clasp it gently in the hand and flatten the end in the crumbs, then turn the hand over and flatten the other end. Now place the croquette in the egg and pour the egg over it with a teaspoon, being careful that every part is covered with the egg, if it is not, the fat will find its way inside and break the croquette open. Remove the croquette from the egg with a wide bladed knife. Next, roll the croquette in the crumbs again and flatten the ends with a knife. After dipping in the egg and crumbs they may stand some time if desired.

To fry them, the fat should be hot enough to brown a piece of bread in forty seconds. Put the croquettes into a frying basket, not having them touch. Lower the basket gently into the fat.

When golden brown the croquettes are done. It should take sixty seconds. Remove them carefully from the basket and drain on brown paper.

Serve on a napkin, with a few sprigs of parsley. The croquettes are improved by using one half sweetbreads or mushrooms.

MUTTON CROQUETTES.

Cooked mutton, 1 pint.
Milk, 1 pint.
Flour, 3 tablespoonfuls.
Butter, 3 tablespoonfuls.
Lemon juice, 2 tablespoonfuls.

Onion juice, 1 teaspoonful.
Salt, 1 tablespoonful.
Pepper, ½ teaspoonful.
Chopped Parsely, 1 tablespoonful.

Prepare, mix, shape and fry like chicken croquettes.

CRÈME FRÊTE.

Milk, 2¼ cups.
Sugar, ½ cup.
Corn starch, 2 tablespoonfuls.
Flour, 1 tablespoonful.
Yolks of eggs, 3.
Stick cinnamon, 1 inch.

Butter, 1 teaspoonful.
Vanilla, 1 teaspoonful.
Salt, 1 saltspoonful.
Eggs, 2.
Crumbs, 1½ cups.

Scald one pint of milk with the cinnamon. Beat together the sugar, corn starch, flour, one-fourth cup milk and yolks of eggs. Add the mixture to the milk and stir till it stiffens. Cook fifteen minutes, then add the butter, vanilla and salt. Remove the cinnamon, and pour into a buttered bread pan, and set away till cold. Then cut it into strips or diamonds, and roll in crumbs and egg, and fry like *croquettes*.

FRITTER BATTER.

Eggs, 2.
Flour, 1 cupful.
Milk, ½ cupful.

Salt, 1 saltspoonful.
Olive oil or melted butter, 1 tablespoonful.

Sift the dry ingredients. Beat the eggs separately. Add the milk to the yolks, and pour onto the flour, making a smooth batter; then add the oil or butter, and beat well. Fold in the whites of the eggs. If the batter is used for meat or for fish add one tablespoonful lemon juice or vinegar, if for fruit use one teaspoonful of sugar

BANANA FRITTERS.

Select ripe bananas, and cut them in two lengthwise, or if very large cut again crossways, spread on a plate and sprinkle with orange or lemon juice and sugar. Let them stand half an hour, and then dip into the batter. Have the batter just cover them, and drop gently into hot fat that will brown a piece of bread in sixty seconds. When brown on one side turn, and when golden brown all over remove with a wire spoon, and drain on brown paper, sprinkle with powdered sugar and serve.

APPLE FRITTERS.

Select sour apples, pare and core them. Cut into quarter inch slices across the apple, leaving the hole in the centre. Spread on a plate, and sprinkle with lemon juice, sugar and cinnamon or nutmeg. Let them stand for half an hour. Fry like banana fritters.

SARDINE CANAPÈS.

Sardines, 12.
Slices of bread, 12.
Cold butter, 1 tablespoonful.
Lemon juice, 2 tablespoonfuls.

Cayenne pepper, 1 saltspoonful.
Hard cooked eggs, 4.
Clarified butter, 4 tablespoonfuls.

Cut the bread into strips three inches long, one and a half inches wide and a quarter of an inch thick Fry till golden in the clarified butter. Remove skin and bones from four sardines, and pound to a paste with the cold butter, one tablespoonful of lemon juice and pepper. Chop the yolks and whites of the egg, separately, very fine. Spread each strip of bread with the sardine paste. Cut the remainder of the sardines into fillets. Put two fillets on each canapè, having them near the edge of the strips of bread, pour a tablespoonful of lemon juice over the fillets. Fill the spaces between the fillets with little mounds of egg, alternating the yolks with the white. Pound all the sardines and eggs together, and spread between two strips of bread, like small sandwiches.

Canapès are served at dinners, luncheons, suppers and garden parties. Serve as a relish with olives.

MEAT AND FISH SAUCES.

Brown Sauce.

Brown stock, 1 pint.
Flour, 2 tablespoonfuls ( ).
Butter, 2 tablespoonfuls.
Chopped onions, 2 tablespoonfuls.
Chopped carrots, 2 tablespoonfu[ls]
Lemon juice, 1 tablespoonful.
Salt, 1 teaspoonful.
Pepper, 1 saltspoonful.

Cook the vegetables in the butter fifteen minute[s,] add the flour, and when as brown as a chestn[ut] draw the pan back and let it cool slightly, then grad[-]ually add the stock, and then the seasoning. S[et] the sauce pan where the sauce will boil slowly [on] one side for twenty minutes. Skim off the f[at,] strain and serve.

Brown Mushroom Sauce.

Add the liquor from a can of mushrooms to t[he] *brown sauce* with the stock. When done add t[he] mushrooms, and cook five minutes longer.

White Sauce.

Milk, 1 pint.
Butter, 2 tablespoonfuls.
Flour, 2 tablespoonfuls.
Salt, 1 teaspoonful.
Pepper, 1 saltspoonful.

SAUCES.

Scald the milk in the double boiler. Put the butter and flour into a. frying pan; when they become smooth and frothy all over the pan, add the milk. Add a little at a time, and let the sauce boil up each time. Stir constantly, and keep the sauce smooth. Be sure that the lumps are smoothed out when it is quite stiff. Let each lot of milk become well blended with the flour before more is added. Add salt and pepper.

This is used for creamed vegetables, escaloped dishes, etc.

Drawn Butter.

Hot stock or water, 1 pint.
Butter, ½ cupful.
Flour, 2 tablespoonfuls.

Salt, ½ teaspoonful.
Pepper, ½ saltspoonful.

Mix like the white sauce. Use half milk if prefered. Use the above for the foundation of the following sauces:

Shrimp Sauce.—Add one cupful of shrimps, chopped fine, one tablespoonful of lemon juice, and a speck of cayenne pepper.

Lobster Sauce.—Put the shells, pounded, and the scraggy parts of a lobster into one and a half pints of cold water, boil half an hour. Strain the water and use for the foundation of the sauce. Add half pint of meat cut into quarter-inch cubes, and the dried and pounded coral, a speck of cayenne pepper, and two tablespoonfuls of lemon juice.

Egg Sauce.—Add three hard cooked eggs, chopped.

Parsely Sauce.—Add two tablespoonfuls of chopped parsley.

Oyster Sauce.—Cook one pint of oysters till plump; drain, and use liquor, for sauce. Add one saltspoonful of celery salt and one speck cayenne pepper, and the yolk of one egg if you like. Add oysters and cook five minutes.

Caper Sauce.—Add three tablespoonfuls of capers and one tablespoonful of lemon juice.

CREAM SAUCE.

Cream, 1 pint.
Butter, 1 tablespoonful.
Flour, 1 tablespoonful.

Salt, 1 teaspoonful.
Pepper, 1 saltspoonful.

Mix like white sauce.

TOMATO SAUCE.

Tomato, 1 pint.
Hot water, ½ pint.
Chopped onion, 1 tablespoonful.
Parsley, 2 sprigs.
Bouquet of sweet herbs.
Peppercorns, 2.

Whole cloves, 2.
Allspice berries, 2.
Butter, 1 tablespoonful.
Flour, 1 "
Salt, 1 teaspoonful.
Pepper, ½ saltspoonful.

Put the tomato, water, herbs, parsley, and spices into a granite sauce pan. Fry the onion in the butter till yellow, add the flour, and when frothy add the tomato. Return to the sauce pan and boil ten minutes and strain.

MINT SAUCE.

Fresh chopped mint, 1 cup. Vinegar, ½ cup.
Sugar, ¼ cup.

Wash, and chop the mint very fine, add sugar and let it stand one hour.

MAÎTRE D' HÔTEL BUTTER.

Butter, ¼ cup. Lemon juice, 1 tablespoonful.
Salt, ½ teaspoonful. Chopped parsley, 1 "
Pepper, ½ saltspoonful.

Cream the butter and add the seasoning, stirring well.

HOLLANDAISE SAUCE.

Buter, ½ cup. Salt, 1 saltspoonful.
Yolks of eggs, 3 or 4. Cayenne pepper, ¼ saltspoonful.
Lemon juice, 1½ tablespoonfuls. Boiling water, ⅓ cup.

Rub the butter to a cream, stir in the yolks of the eggs unbeaten, one at a time, and beat well, add the seasoning and then beat with a Dover beater for five minutes. Add the boiling water. Set the bowl into a sauce pan of boiling water and stir till it stiffens, like a soft custard. Remove immediately when done or it will curdle.

Bread Sauce.

Milk, 1 pint.
Sifted crumbs, ⅓ cup.
Coarse crumbs, ⅔ cup.
Butter, 2 tablespoonfuls.

Onions, ¼.
Salt, 1 teaspoonful.
Pepper, 1 saltspoonful.

Cook the milk, fine crumbs, and onion in the double boiler fifteen minutes. Remove the onion and add one tablespoonful of butter, salt and pepper. Serve this with game. Brown the coarse crumbs in the remainder of the butter, and when brown throw over the roasted birds.

VEGETABLES.

GENERAL DIRECTIONS FOR BOILING VEGETABLES.

Vegetables, such as turnips, onions, carrots, parsnips, cabbage, cauliflower, rice macaroni, and spaghetti, should be cooked in a large quantity of boiling water, at least four times the quantity of vegetables. Salt should be added when about half done.

A saltspoonful of soda added to one quart of beans, peas, cabbage, etc., will make them more tender and preserve the color.

Boil vegetables steadily the whole time. Do not let them stand in warm water.

Drain all vegetables as soon as cooked. They deteriorate rapidly by over cooking, but should always be cooked till tender.

They may be served simply with salt, butter and pepper, or with a white sauce.

The *time* of cooking depends upon the *age*, *size*, and quality of the vegetables. The older the vegetables the longer time they require. Fresh summer vegetables will cook in half the time required by those which have been gathered several days.

VEGETABLES.

Here is a time-table giving the approximate time required for boiling vegetables:

Fresh green corn, five minutes; older or wilted corn, ten minutes.

Peas, asparagus, potatoes, rice, celery, spinach, canned tomatoes, summer squash, thirty minutes.

Macaroni, young beets, young carrots, young turnips, young onions, young parsnips, sweet potatoes, canned corn, young cabbage, thirty to forty-five minutes.

Shell beans, oyster plant, winter squash, spaghetti, cauliflower, forty-five minutes to one hour.

Winter carrots, winter turnips, Bermuda onions, winter parsnips, string beans, one hour to two hours.

String beans, two to three hours.

Old beets, *forever*.

BOILED POTATOES.

Potatoes, 12.
Boiling water, 2 quarts.
Salt, 1 tablespoonful.

Wash, pare and soak the potatoes in cold water from fifteen minutes to two hours, according to the age of the potatoes. The older the potatoes the longer they should soak. Cover with the boiling water and boil fifteen minutes, then add the salt and boil fifteen minutes longer. Pour off every drop of the water and shake over the stove till dry

VEGETABLES.

and floury. If they are to stand before serving, cover with a towel.

MASHED POTATOES.

Boiled potatoes, 12. Salt, 1 tablespoonful.
Scalded milk, ½ cup. Butter, 1 "

Mash the potatoes with a wire masher as soon as they are boiled, in a hot sauce pan. When fine and light, add the butter and salt. Then add the milk gradually, beating well. When all is added, beat with a spoon till very light and white. Be sure that the potato is kept hot and that the milk is hot.

POTATO PUFFS.

Hot mashed potatoes, 1 pint. Parsley, 1 teaspoonful.
Egg, 1.

Prepare as for mashed potato, add the parsley chopped, and nearly all of the egg, well beaten. Shape into small, flattish balls. Place on a buttered tin sheet, and brush over the top with the remainder of the egg. Bake till light brown in a hot oven. Or put the potato through a pastry bag, forming fancy shapes. These make a pretty garnish for meat dishes.

Lyonnaise Potatoes.

Cold boiled potatoes, 1 quart.
Chopped onion, 1 tablespoonful.
Butter, 3 "
Chopped parsley, 1 tablespoonful.
Salt, 1 teaspoonful.
Pepper, 1 saltspoonful.

Cut the potatoes into one-half inch cubes, sprinkle with salt and pepper. Fry the onion in the butter till yellow. Put in the potatoes and cook till hot and slightly browned, add the parsley and serve.

Potato a la Maître d' Hôtel.

Cooked potatoes, 1 quart.
Milk, 1 pint.
Butter, 3 tablespoonfuls.
Yolks of eggs, 2.
Flour, 1 teaspoonful.
Salt, 1 teaspoonful.
Pepper, 1 saltspoonful.
Lemon juice, 1 teaspoonful.
Chopped parsley, 1 tablespoonful.

Cut the potatoes into one-half inch cubes, sprinkle with salt and pepper. Put into the double boiler with the milk. Cook ten minutes. Cream the butter, add eggs, flour, lemon juice, and parsley, then stir into the potatoes and cook five minutes, stirring carefully to keep the potatoes in whole pieces.

Creamed Potatoes.

Cut one quart of cooked potatoes into one-half inch cubes, season with salt and pepper. Cook in one pint of cream sauce for one-half hour in the double boiler.

VEGETABLES.

Escaloped Potatoes.

Turn the *creamed potatoes* into a buttered escaloped dish. Cover with one-half cupful of sifted crumbs, moistened with one tablespoonful of melted butter, and bake twenty minutes.

Baked Potatoes.

Scrub the potatoes with a brush. Put them into a hot oven, bake forty-five minutes, or till as soft as a mellow apple. Then break the skin to let out the steam, wrap in a napkin and serve immediately.

Creamed Vegetables.

Creamed carrots, creamed onions, creamed cauliflower, creamed cabbage and creamed parsnips are prepared in nearly the same way. Cut the carrots and parsnips into one-half inch cubes and boil by the directions given, till perfectly tender. Boil one onion with one quart of carrots, mash the onions, and break the cauliflower into small pieces. Add to one quart of these cooked vegetables, one pint of White Sauce Add more salt and pepper, if needed.

Escaloped Vegetables.

These same vegetables are very nice escaloped.

Turn the vegetables as prepared in the above recipe, into a buttered escaloped dish, with alternate layers of white sauce, using just enough sauce to moisten them. Cover with one-half cup of sifted crumbs moistened with one tablespoonful of melted butter. Bake one-half hour.

To Boil Cabbage.

To boil a cabbage so that it will not fill the house with an unpleasant odor, follow these directions exactly.

Wash the cabbage under the faucet and drain in a colander. Have a large kettle nearly full of water boiling rapidly, break off the leaves from the cabbage, one at a time, and drop them into the water, add one tablespoonful of salt and one saltspoonful of soda, keep the water boiling rapidly all the time and the cover off. A fresh cabbage will cook in one-half hour.

Escaloped Tomatoes.

Tomatoes, 1 quart.
Stale bread, 1 pint.
Bread crumbs, ½ cup.
Butter, 3 tablespoonfuls.

Salt, 1 tablespoonful.
Pepper, ½ saltspoonful.
Sugar, 1 teaspoonful.

Use fresh or canned tomatoes. Butter an escaloped dish. Mix the seasoning with the tomatoes. Put in a layer of tomatoes, then one of the bread broken into bits, then a few bits of butter, and so continue till the dish is full, using two tablespoonfuls of the butter. Moisten the sifted crumbs with the remainder of the butter melted and put on the top, or stale bread may be used for all. More butter may be used if wished richer.

Baked Macaroni.

Macaroni, ¼ lb.
Whith sauce, 1 pint.
Grated cheese, 1 cup.

Bread crumbs, 1 cup.
Butter, 2 tablespoonfuls.

Butter an escaloped dish, put in a layer of the sauce, then one of boiled macaroni, cut into six inch pieces. Sprinkle with cheese, and so continue till all the materials are used. Melt the butter, stir in the crumbs, spread on the top of the macaroni, and bake one-half hour.

Spaghetti.

Prepare like macaroni, substituting the spaghetti for the macaroni, and one pint of tomato sauce for the white sauce. Serve on a platter.

Turkish Pilaf.

Strained and seasoned tomato, 1 cup.
Stock, 1 cup.
Rice, ⅔ cup.

Butter, ½ cup.
Salt, 1 teaspoonful.
Pepper, ¼ teaspoonful.

Boil one pint of tomato with one chopped onion, one sprig of parsley, two cloves and two peppercorns for ten minutes and strain. This gives the one cup of tomato. Wash the rice through three waters, then boil in one quart of water for five minutes, and drain. Put the rice into the double boiler, add tomato, stock, salt and pepper. Steam one hour, or till the rice is tender, add the butter, in small bits, on the top, Do not stir. Remove the cover and cover with a towel. Let it stand ten minutes, and serve.

Macédoine of Vegetables.

French peas, 1 can, or
Fresh peas, 1 quart.
Carrot cubes, 1 pint.
Turnip   "   1 pint, or
Potato balls, 1 quart.

Stock, 3 gills.
Butter, 3 teaspoonfuls.
Sugar, 3   "
Salt, 3   "

Put the vegetables into separate sauce pans, add two quarts of boiling water and cook till tender. If canned peas are used, drain them and pour cold water on them. When tender drain off the water from each vegetable, and add to each, one-third of the butter, salt, and sugar and stock.

Boil rapidly till the stock is absorbed. If potatoes are used omit the sugar and stock and add one tablespoonful of butter.

Spread the turnips on a warm platter, having a

border rather thick and the thickness decrease toward the center of the platter.

Heap the carrots on the turnips covering all but a border one inch wide.. Flatten the carrots and heap the peas upon them.

If potatoes are used in place of turnips, cut them in balls or cubes, boil for ten minutes and drain, season with one teaspoonful of salt, one Tablespoonful of butter.

SALADS.

Mayonnaise Dressing.

Mustard, 1 tablespoonful.
Sugar, 1 "
Cayenne pepper, 2 specks.
Salt, 1 teaspoonful.
Yolks of eggs, 3.

Salad oil, 1 pint.
Vinegar, ¼ cup.
Lemons, ½ or 1.
Whipped cream, 1 cup.

Mix the dry ingredients with the yolks of the egg in a quart bowl. Beat with the large sized Dover beater till thick. Now add the oil, one teaspoonful or so, at a time, not more, till the mixture is so thick that it can be taken upon the beater, then add a few drops of vinegar, which will thin it; then continue with the oil, adding it more rapidly, and so on till oil and vinegar are used. Then add the lemon juice. Just before serving *fold* in the whipped cream. The cream may be omitted and beaten whites of eggs substituted, but it is not so nice.

Boiled Dressing.

Mustard, 1 teaspoonful.
Salt, 2 "
Cayenne pepper, ¼ saltspoonful.
Sugar, 2 tablespoonfuls.

Vinegar, ½ cup.
Cream or milk, 1 cup.
Melted butter or oil, 2 tablespoonfuls.

Mix the dry ingredients, and moisten with the vinegar, pour on to the beaten eggs, stirring as you do so. Add the cream and then the butter. Place the bowl in a pan of boiling water and stir till it thickens. Remove from the water, strain, and set away till cold.

Sour Cream Dressing.

Mustard, 1 teaspoonful.
Salt, 1   "
Vinegar, 3 tablespoonfuls.
Eggs, 1.
Melted butter, 1 tablespoonful.
Sour cream, 3   "

Mix the salt and mustard, add the vinegar and stir till smooth. Beat the egg and add the vinegar, stirring all the time, and then the butter. Set the bowl into a pan of boiling water and cook till it thickens. Remove from the fire and set away till cold. The richer the cream the better. If it is clabbered, stir it in. If it is not, whip with the Dover beater till stiff and then *fold* it in. If the cream is very rich the butter may be omitted.

French Dressing.

Salt. 1 saltspoonful.
Pepper, ½   "
Vinegar, 1 tablespoonful.
Oil, 3   "

Mix the salt and pepper, add one tablespoonful of oil. Stir and then add vinegar and the remainder of the oil. A few drops of onion juice may be added.

Chicken Salad.

Remove skin, fat, gristle and bones from cold cooked chicken and cut into one-quarter inch cubes. To one quart of this chicken add a marinade made by mixing three tablespoonfuls of vinegar, one tablespoonful of oil, one teaspoonful of salt, one-half teaspoonful of pepper. Mix well and set away in the refrigerator for two or three hours.

Cut in thin slices enough tender, white celery to make one pint. Wash in cold water, put in a bowl with some ice on top and set away in the refrigerator. At serving time, not before, drain the celery and mix with the chicken. Moisten with mayonnaise or sour cream dressing and turn into a salad bowl. Spread one-half pint or so of dressing over the top. Garnish with some of the blanched celery leaves and olives.

Shrimp Salad.

If canned shrimps are used, rinse them in cold water and drain. If fresh ones are used, shell them. Cut into one-half inch cubes and sprinkle over them a marinade made by mixing one-half teaspoonful of salt, one-quarter teaspoonful of pepper, one tablespoonful of oil, and two tablespoonfuls of vinegar and one of lemon juice. Place in the refrigerator for two or three hours.

Take the tender heart leaves from three or four heads of lettuce. Wash them and place in a pan with some pieces of ice. Set in the ice box till crispy.

At serving time shake away moisture from the leaves and arrange in the form of shells by putting two or three leaves together. Moisten the shrimps with mayonnaise or sour cream dressing, and place a heaping teaspoonful in each shell, and one teaspoonful of dressing on top. Garnish with capers and bits of lettuce leaves or parsley. The shrimps are sometimes left whole.

Vegetable Salad.

Cold boiled potatoes, 1 quart.	Chopped onion, 1 tablespoonful.
Cold boiled beets, 1 cup.	" celery, ½ cup.
Cold boiled carrots, ½ cup.	Hard cooked eggs, 2.
Chopped parsley, 1 tablespoonful.	French dressing.

Cut the vegetables into one-half inch cubes or into fancy shapes with vegetable cutters. Sprinkle with one teaspoonful of salt and one-half teaspoonful of pepper. Chop the onion very fine and mix with twice the recipe of French Dressing. Chop the whites of the eggs. Mix the vegetables in alternate layers on a platter or salad bowl, moistening each layer with the dressing. Rub the yolks of eggs through a strainer. Reserve some nice pieces of beet for the top, and throw over the whole some of the chopped parsley and yolks of egg.

Garnish with sprigs of parsley or blanched celery leaves. The amount and variety of vegetables may be varied by the taste and season. Sour cream or boiled dressing may be used in place of French Dressing.

MARGUERITE SALAD.

Arrange sixteen small, crisp leaves of lettuce on a platter, putting two leaves together to make a shell. Cut the whites of eight hard cooked eggs into rings and mash the yolks and moisten with mayonnaise boiled, or sour cream dressing. Place the white rings on the lettuce for the petals of the daisy and the yolks in the center.

Serve more dressing with the salad.

BREAKFAST AND TEA DISHES.

Plain Omelet.

Eggs, 4.   Milk, 4 tablespoonfuls.
Salt, ½ teaspoonful.   Butter, 1 teaspoonful.

Beat the eggs till well broken but not light, add the salt and milk. Put a small French frying pan where it will heat slowly, and a small platter to heat in the oven. Rub the butter around in the pan and when hot, turn in the egg. Shake the pan vigorously to keep the egg moving, and when thick and creamy tip the pan from you, and with a knife roll up the omelet away from you. Let it rest in the pan for one half minute, to brown on the bottom; then take the pan in the right hand, and the platter in the left, and turn the omelet into the platter. Serve immediately.

Light Omelet.

Use the same quantities as for Plain Omelet. Beat the eggs separately till very light. Add salt and milk to the yolks and *fold* in the whites. Turn into the hot buttered pan, cover with a hot cover and remove toward the back of the stove. When stiff and dry in the center or in about four or five minutes, place in the top of the oven to dry the top, then fold into one half the pan, and turn out onto the hot platter.

Egg Vermicelli.

Eggs, 3.	Pepper, ½ saltspoonful
Milk, 1 cup.	Flour, 1 teaspoonful.
Salt, ½ teaspoonful.	Butter, 1 teaspoonful.

Cook the eggs hard. Chop the whites fine, mash the yolks, and add one saltspoonful of mustard, a speck of cayenne pepper, one-half saltspoonful of salt, and one tablespoonful of cream. Cook the butter and flour till smooth and frothy, and then add the milk gradually, and the salt, pepper, and whites of eggs. Cut six rounds of toast with a cutter. Pile the whites of eggs on them and pour the sauce around. Mash the yolks through a strainer over the whites. Garnish with points of toast and parsley.

Egg Baskets.

Eggs, 3.	Salt, ½ teaspoonful.
Chopped cooked meat, 3 tablespoonfuls.	Pepper, 1 saltspoonful.
Melted butter, 1 tablespoonful.	Mustard, 1 saltspoonful.

Cook the eggs hard. Cut in two crossways and cut a thin slice from each end so that the eggs may stand upright, and place on a platter. Remove the yolks, add the meat, which should be chicken, veal or ham, and chopped very fine, butter, seasoning and cream enough to hold the mixture in shape. Mash till smooth. Make into balls the size of the original yolks, and place in the white cups. Pour one cupful of the white sauce around them, and set in the oven for five minutes, then place a tiny sprig of parsley in the top of each, and serve,

Escaloped Eggs.

Eggs. 6.
White sauce, 1 pint.
Cracker crumbs, 1 cup.

Butter, ¼ cup.
Cold meat, 1 cup.

Cook the eggs hard. Chop the ham, tongue fish or chicken, very fine. Moisten the crumbs with the butter, melted. Make the white sauce from milk, cream, or stock. Chop the whites of the eggs, and put the yolks through a strainer. Make alternate layers of the sauce, crumbs, whites and yolks, putting crumbs on the top. Bake till the mixture is heated through and the crumbs are brown.

Baked Eggs.

Small shallow dishes, of various shapes and qualities, come on purpose for serving baked, or shirred eggs, and there are many ways of serving.

No. 1. Butter an egg dish and break an egg into it, being careful not to break the yolk. Sprinkle with salt and pepper and bake till the white is jelly-like. Place a bit of butter on the top of the egg and serve. Or they may be baked on a platter in the same way. Place a strip of broiled or fried breakfast bacon on the top of each egg, for a variety.

No. 2. Sprinkle the dishes with seasoned and buttered cracker, or bread crumbs, drop in the egg, cover with crumbs and bake till the white is jelly-like and the crumbs are brown.

No. 3. A great variety of flavors may be given to the eggs by preparing in either of the preceding ways, and spreading one of the following in the dish before the egg is dropped:—A few drops of onion juice; one teaspoonful of chopped parsley; one teaspoonful of finely chopped cooked ham, or one teaspoonful of grated cheese.

No. 4. Beat two or three extra whites of eggs to a stiff froth, season with a sprinkle of salt, and spread it on a platter, making little hollows like nests, in it, or one nest in each little dish. Break a whole egg into the nest, and bake as before.

Hard Cooked Eggs.

Put the eggs into a covered sauce pan containing enough boiling water to cover the eggs. Set

BREAKFAST AND TEA DISHES.

the sauce pan where the water will keep hot but not boil, for twenty minutes. This will give a more digestible egg than one boiled for ten minutes.

Soft Cooked Eggs.

Place the eggs in water as for Hard Cooked Eggs, and let them remain there for five or ten minutes, as they are liked soft or stiff. The less an egg is cooked the more digestible it is. The white should be like a jelly.

Tea.

Allow one teaspoonful of tea and one-half pint of *fresh* boiling water to each person. Scald the tea pot and put in the tea, let it stand on the stove for a minute, then add the water. Let it *steep* but *not boil*, from three to five minutes.

Boiled Coffee.

Mix one cup of ground coffee with one egg and one-half cup of cold water. Scald the coffee pot and pour in the coffee mixture and add one quart and one cup of *fresh* boiling water. Close the coffee pot tightly, and just bring the coffee to a boil; then place it at the back of the stove where it will keep just below the boiling point, for ten minutes. Then pour out a cupful to clear the nozzle, and turn back, add one-half cupful of cold water and in a minute it is ready to serve. Serve with scalded milk and cream.

Chocolate.

Put one quart of milk into the double boiler.

Scrape two ounces of Baker's chocolate and put into a granite sauce pan, with four tablespoonfuls of hot water and two tablespoonfuls of sugar. Cook till smooth and glossy, then add the milk, which should be scalded. Add a little at a time. When the sauce pan is full and all has boiled up once, return to the double boiler. Serve for lunch with whipped cream. One-half water may be used, and one-half as much chocolate, if desired less rich.

The Mixing of Batters.

A *true batter* is of such consistency as will allow of pouring. It should not drop from the spoon, yet it must not run like a mere liquid. For this measure a scant measure of liquid to a full one of flour. A *cream batter* is the consistency of rich cream. For this use full measure of liquid to full measure of flour.

A *semi-dough* or *drop batter*, is one which will not pour but will break from the spoon. For this take three-quarter measure of liquid to one measure of flour. A *dough*, to be stiff enough to knead and handle, should be pliable and soft, rather than hard. For this take half measure scant of liquid to one full measure of flour.

Sift the flour before measuring.

To "beat eggs separately" beat the yolks and whites in separate bowls.

In mixing a batter, get the materials called for, together, and measure them, then mix in the following order, unless directions to the contrary are given:

Sift the dry ingredients into the mixing bowl and mix well. Beat the eggs separately. Add the milk to the yolks. Pour this liquor onto the dry ingredients, and beat well. When light, add the butter, melted, or it is sometimes mixed with the dry flour at the first. This is supposing a small amount of butter, as in muffins, not for cake. *Fold* in the whites of the eggs the last thing.

Baking Powders.

The object of using soda and cream of tartar or baking powder in batter is to make them light. Bicarbonate of soda and cream of tartar when dissolved and heated, unite and form Rochelle salt, water and carbonic acid gas. The carbonic acid gas generated through the batter, rises and puffs it up, making a light, porous mass, in which condition we bake it. The Rochelle salt is left in the batter. We have various kinds of baking powders. The most are made from soda and tartaric acid, soda and cream of tartar, soda and alum, or soda and acid phosphate. These all give off carbonic acid gas in varying proportions, but leave each a different residue in the batter.

The cream of tartar baking powders are the most wholesome. The others are undesirable from a healthful point of view.

Measure soda level, and the cream of tartar a little rounding, baking powder, rounding.

Allow two teaspoonfuls of cream of tartar to one teaspoonful of soda.

When you wish to use baking powder in place of soda and cream of tartar, given; use as much baking powder as the soda and cream of tartar added together.

When baking powder is given and you wish to substitute soda and cream of tartar, use two-thirds cream of tartar, and one-third soda.

Allow one level teaspoonful of baking powder to every cup of flour.

Allow one teaspoonful of soda to one pint of sour, clabbered milk.

Allow one teaspoonful of soda to one cup of molasses.

BAKING POWDER BISCUIT.

Flour, 1 quart.
Salt, 1 teaspoonful.
Baking powder, 3 teaspoonfuls.

Butter, 1 tablespoonful.
Milk, about 1 pint.

Sift the dry ingredients. Rub in the butter with the tips of the fingers till all the lumps disappear. Mix in the milk gradually, cutting it with a knife. Mix only a small part of the flour with each addion of the milk. Mix as little as possible, and when just stiff enough to handle turn out on to a floured board.

Toss it with the knife till floured all over, then pat it out with the hands till one-half inch thick. Handle as little as possible. Cut with a round cutter and place on a tin sheet and bake at once in a *very* hot oven.

Strawberry Short Cake.

Like the above, only substitute rich, sour cream for the milk, and use one scant teaspoonful of soda in place of baking powder. Or, like baking powder biscuit, only use one-half cup of butter in place of one tablespoonful.

Bake in Washingtonpie plates thin, and put two together, or bake thick and when they come from the oven slip a thin, sharp knife between the cake and the pan and when hot, split the cake.

For the filling.—Mash one quart of strawberries in an earthen dish, and mix in sugar till of a pleasant sweetness. Set the dish in the oven till the fruit is scalded, no longer. Butter each half of the short cake, pour on some of the berries, cover with the top and pour the remainder of the fruit over it. Sprinkle with sugar and serve.

Or, the berries may be used without the cooking.

ORANGE SHORT CAKE.

Prepare the same as strawberry short cake, using oranges. Peel them and remove the thick under skin and seeds. Sweeten to taste and spread on the cakes. Fresh or canned peaches may be used, and raspberries as a filling for a short cake.

CREAM WAFFLES.

Butter, ½ cup.
Cream, ½ pint.
Milk, ½ pint.

Flour, 1 pint.
Salt, ½ teaspoonful,
Eggs, 4.

Cream the butter, add the well beaten yolks and salt and beat two minutes or more. Now add the flour, milk and cream alternately making a smooth batter. Then beat the whites of the eggs to a stiff dry froth and beat them in.

Have the waffle iron hot and grease it with salt pork. Fill one half of it with the batter and brown it. Bake in all about two minutes. Serve with syrup, or butter and sugar. Some like the addition of cinnamon.

BREAKFAST AND TEA DISHES. 75

SALLY LUNNS. (Raised with Yeast.)

Flour, 1 pint.
Milk, 1 cup.
Sugar, 1 teaspoonful to 2 tablespoonfuls.

Salt, ½ teaspoonful..
Yeast, ¼ cup.
Eggs, 1.
Butter, 1 tablespoonful.

Scald and cool the milk and add the sugar, salt and yeast. Pour on to the egg well beaten and add to the flour, making a smooth batter. Use the larger quantity of sugar, if for tea. Mix late in the forenoon, if for tea, and when risen double in bulk add the butter, melted, and fill muffin pans two-thirds full. Let this rise twenty or thirty minutes, and bake in a hot oven fifteen or twenty minutes. If for breakfast, mix the flour, yeast, salt and milk, late in the evening before. In the morning add egg and melted butter. These may be baked on a hot griddle in muffinn rings, or in one large loaf like sponge cake, or in a pudding dish.

SALLY LUNNS. (Raised with Baking Powder.)

Flour, 1 pint.
Baking powder, 1½ teaspoonfuls.
Salt, ½ teaspoonful.
Sugar, 2 tablespoonfuls.

Milk, ½ cup.
Eggs, 2.
Butter, ¼ to ½ cup.

Sift the dry ingredients into a bowl. Beat the eggs separately. Add the milk to the yolks and pour on to the dry ingredients, beat well, add the butter melted, and beat again, then fold in the whites and fill muffin pans two-thirds full. Bake fifteen minutes in a hot oven. When the one-quarter cup of butter is used add a scant one-quarter cup of milk.

Sponge Corn Cake.

Corn meal, 1 cup,	Butter, ½ cup.
Flour, 2 cups.	Sugar, 1 cup.
Soda, 1 teaspoonful.	Eggs, 3.
Salt, 1 "	Rich sour milk, 2 cups.

Cream the butter till very light.

Beat the eggs separately.

Beat the yolks and whites together. then scatter in the sugar, beating all the while. Sift the dry ingredients. Drop the creamed butter into the center of the flour, turn in the eggs and beat to a batter in the middle. As this mixes add the sour milk, stirring rapidly and keeping the batter soft and light.

Bake one-half hour in gem tins, rings, or Washington pie plates.

Less sugar and butter may be used when desired, but keep the batter the same stiffness.

Graham Muffins.

Graham flour, 1½ pints.	Baking powder, 3 teaspoonfuls.
White flour, 1 cup.	Milk, 1 pint.
Sugar, ½ cup.	Eggs, 2
Salt, 1 teaspoonful.	

Put the Graham flour into a bowl. Sift the remainder of the dry ingredients into it. Beat the eggs light and add the milk. Stir into the dry ingredients and beat well. Grease hot gem pans and fill them two-thirds full. Bake in a hot oven fifteen minutes.

SPIDER CAKE.

Corn meal, ¾ cup.
Flour, ¼ cup.
Sugar, 1 tablespoonful.
Salt, ½ teaspoonful.
Soda, ½ teaspoonful, scant.

Eggs, 1.
Sour milk, ½ cupful.
Sweet milk, 1 cupful.
Butter, 1 tablespoonful.

Sift the dry ingredients into a bowl. Beat the eggs and add one half the sweet milk. Pour onto the dry ingredients. Beat well, then add the sour milk. Put the butter into a *hot* spider, and when hot pour in the batter. Pour the other one-half cup of the milk over the top *without stirring*. Bake twenty or thirty minutes in a hot oven.

RYE MUFFINS.

Rry flour or meal, 1 cup.
White flour, 1 cup.
Sugar, ¼ cup.
Salt, ½ teaspoonful.

Baking powder, 2 teaspoonfuls.
Milk, 1 cup.
Egg, 1.

Sift the dry ingredients. Beat the eggs and add the milk to them and stir quickly into the dry mixture. Bake in hot gem or muffin pans twenty or thirty minutes.

BREAD.

There is so much of interest and use to be said about bread that it is difficult to condense to the necessary limits of these pages. I will briefly outline the process which takes place in the raising and baking, and give a few general directions for making.

Yeast is one of the lowest orders of vegetable organisms. It consists of minute microscopic cells, which under certain conditions multiply very rapidly.

When yeast is added to warmed water and flour it causes the alcoholic fermentation.

The yeast acts upon the starch, some of which is changed into sugar.

$$\underset{\text{Starch.}}{C_6H_{10}O_5} + \underset{\text{Water.}}{H_2O} = \underset{\text{Sugar.}}{C_6H_{12}O_6}$$

Then the sugar is changed into alcohol and carbonic acid gas.

$$\underset{\substack{\text{Sugar}\\C_6H_{12}O_6}}{} = \begin{cases} 2C_2H_6O\ (\text{Alcohol}) \\ 2CO_2\ (\text{Carbonic Acid Gas}) \end{cases}$$

It is for this carbonic acid gas, which causes the sponge-like condition of the bread, that we use the yeast.

The carbonic acid gas generated through the dough, being lighter than the air rises, and in trying to escape, expands the dough and puffs it up to two or three times its original size. The tenacity and elasticity of the gluten prevents the gas from escaping. The dough is baked and the cell walls stiffened in this condition and we have the light porous loaf which is so desirable. If the dough is allowed to get too warm or rise too much, the alcoholic fermentation changes to the acetic and sour bread is the result.

$$C_2H_6O + O_2 = C_2H_4O_2 + H_2O.$$
Alcohol. Acetic Acid.

The temperature of the dough is very important. The best temperature for the first rising is 70° to 75°, the maximum 90°.

At a higher temperature the acetic acid is liable to be formed. After the dough has once begun to rise it will continue, though more slowly, though the temperature be lowered to 40°.

The denser the dough the more yeast is needed and the more slowly it rises.

A dough containing eggs and butter will rise more slowly than one which does not. Just before the baking of the bread the temperature may be raised considerably without injury, as the heat of the oven so soon checks the rising.

The first kneading of the bread is to mix the yeast thoroughly through the dough. The second kneading, that the bubbles of gas may be broken into small ones, and so make the bread fine grained.

The object of baking is to kill the yeast, cook the starch, expand the carbonic acid gas and drive off the alcohol. Some of the starch on the outside is decomposed by the intense heat, changing it to dextrine. This gives the sweet crust.

The compressed yeast cakes, "Fleischmann's" or the "Vienna" or a nice home made yeast, are the best. A general rule is one-half cup of yeast to one pint of liquid. One-half cake of compressed yeast dissolved in one cup of luke-warm water is equal to one cup of yeast. Mix bread with milk or water. It is mostly a matter of taste or economy which is the best. When milk is used always scald it and cool to 90°. A general rule is one scant measure of liquid, including the yeast, to three full measures of flour. Mix bread with a liquid at 90° in cool weather, with a cold one in summer.

Knead till soft and smooth the first time, till soft and elastic the second. Use as little flour as possible during the second kneading. The bread should rise till doubled in bulk. It should not rise till it caves in or runs over the bowl.

When risen, "cut it down" by cutting it away from the sides of the bowl and working it into the centre. Repeat this several times if necessary before you are ready to shape it into loaves.

Let rolls rise more than loaves before baking, for the heat soon penetrates to the centre and stops the rising, but a loaf will rise more after being put in the oven.

The oven for baking should be hot enough to raise the inside of the loaf to 212° or between 400° and 500°. It should brown one tablespoonful of flour in five minutes.

Allow fifteen minutes for the baking of single rolls.

Thirty minutes for a sheet of rolls.

Forty-five and fifty minutes for a loaf.

A loaf of bread when done should be brown all over, and give a hollow sound when hit with the knuckles.

Spread the bread with melted butter before placing in the oven and it will have a very soft, brown crust, spread with water, or milk and sugar and it will be shiny. Brush with egg and it will have a golden brown, shiny crust. Wash the top of loaves with cold water when they come from the oven and return till dry and they have a dark, shiny crust.

If you wish a soft crust wrap the bread with a clean, thick linnen cloth while hot. If a crispy crust is liked, let the bread cool first. Keep it in a clean jar or box. This should be scalded and dried and freed from crusts and crumbs often.

YEAST.

Water, 2 quarts.
Hops, 2 tablespoonfuls.
Raw potatoes, 6.

Sugar, ½ cup.
Salt, ¼ cup.
Yeast, 1 cup.

Put the water and hops on to boil. Grate the potatoes into an earthen bowl. Strain the hop water over them before they blacken. Place on the stove and boil up once, and then add salt and sugar. Let it cool till blood warm, and then add the yeast. Let it rise in a temperature between 70° and 90° for five or six hours, when it should look white and frothy. Turn into a stone jug, cork tightly, and keep in a cool place.

Scald the jug and the stopper thoroughly each time the jug is emptied.

WHITE BREAD.

Milk, or water, or the two mixed, 1 pint.
Sugar, 1 tablespoonful.
Salt, 1 teaspoonful.

Yeast, ½ cup.
Flour, 6 cups or more.
If water is used, use
Butter, or lard, 1 tablespoonful.

Scald the milk and cool to 100°F, add sugar, salt and yeast. When shortening is used add it to the hot milk, or when water alone is used spread the shortening over the dough after the first kneading and it is put into the bowl. This is to prevent the hard, dry crust from forming on the top. Stir the flour into the liquid with a strong knife or perforated wooden spoon. Add flour till stiff enough to knead. The quantity will vary with the brand of flour used.

Take the dough on to the board and knead till smooth and elastic. Return to the bowl, add the shortening if not already used. Cover with a thick bread cloth kept for the purpose, and a tin cover. Let it rise till doubled in bulk; cut it down, knead again, and shape into loaves. Place in buttered pans. Let it rise till doubled in bulk. Bake from forty-five to sixty minutes.

GRAHAM BREAD.

In mixing remove one pint of the "white bread" dough when almost as stiff as a drop batter, and let it rise in another bowl. When very light and full of bubbles, dissolve one scant teaspoonful of soda in one-quarter cup of cold water, add this to one cup of molasses, and when well mixed add to the dough. Stir till smooth then add one cup of warm water. Now stir in Graham flour till stiff enough to handle. Flour the board and shape into loaves or biscuit. Do not knead or handle only enough to get it into shape. Let it rise till double in bulk. Bake a little longer than the same size loaf of white bread. Diminish the heat of the oven when half done.

One-fourth of a cup of sugar may be used instead of molasses.

In that case omit the soda and add one cup of water.

WHITE MOUNTAIN ROLLS.

Milk, 1 pint.
Butter, ½ cup.
Sugar, ¼ cup.
Salt, 1 teasponful.

Yeast, ½ cup,
Whites of eggs, 2.
Flour, 7 or 8 cups,

Scald the milk, and add butter, sugar, salt. Let it cool to 100°F and then add yeast and whites of eggs beaten. Add the flour till a stiff dough is made and knead till smooth. Let it rise till doubled in bulk. Then, knead again and shape into cylindrical rolls, and place side by side in shallow pans. Let them rise till doubled in bulk, and bake thirty minutes in hot oven.

SWEDISH ROLLS.

Make like White Mountain Rolls, and when ready to shape, roll out on a board till one-eighth inch thick. Spread with soft butter, and sprinkle with sugar and cinnamon. Roll up like a jelly roll, and then cut across in one-half-inch slices. Let them rise till light and bake about ten minutes.

For the following receipts for Swedish Rolls note these directions:

To freshen the butter, melt it, and when a little cool pour off the clear liquid from the salt, which settles at the bottom, or, wash it in cold water. When the butter is to be mixed with egg the first way is easier.

Take the dough after the first rising, knead and mix thoroughly.

Give each roll plenty of room on the tin so that they will not run together. Bake in a hot oven till nicely browned all over.

GIFFLES.

White bread dough, ½ lb. Sugar, ½ tablespoonful.
Freshened butter, 1½ oz.

Take the white bread, (which should be mixed with milk), after the first rising, knead it a little, and then roll out, spread with the butter, fold up the edges, folding the butter in the inside. Fold it up like pastry and roll out three times, till the butter is well mixed into the dough. Then add the sugar and when well mixed roll out till one-eighth inch thick. Cut into eight equal square pieces. Place a bit of jelly a little way from one corner and fold the corner over it. Then roll up towards the opposite corner, making a crescent-shaped roll. Let them rise till nearly doubled, then brush over with one egg mixed with one tablespoonful of water, and sprinkle with sugar. Bake in a hot oven about ten minutes. They should be light brown when done.

SOFT KRINGLES.

White bread dough, ½ lb.
Eggs, 2.
Sugar, 2 heaping tablespoonfuls.
Freshened butter, 2 oz.
Cardamon seeds, 2.

Crush the cardamon seeds in the sugar till fine. Beat the yolks of the eggs, and add the sugar and butter, with flour enough to make the mixture so stiff that it can be kneaded into the dough. Spread out the dough, and add the egg mixture by spoonfuls and knead till there are no streaks of yellow. Roll into long sticks, and then shape into rings. Let them rise till doubled, and bake.

ROLL PETITS.

Soft kringle dough, ½ lb.
Plain bread dough, ¼ lb.
Sugar, 1 tablespoonful.

Knead the two very thoroughly, and shape into small, round rolls. Let them rise till doubled, and bake.

PRUNE KRINGLES.

White bread dough, ½ lb.
Freshened butter, ½ oz.
Sugar, ½ tablespoonful.

Knead the butter and sugar into the dough. Chop six or eight prunes in four tablespoonfuls of sugar, till quite fine. Chop the meat of the stones with the prunes. Spread this on the board. Roll into sticks the size of the finger and eight inches long. Roll in the prunes and sugar till dusted all over, then fasten into oblong rings.

SUGAR KRINGLES.

White bread dough, ½ lb.
Freshened butter, ½ oz.
Sugar, ½ tablespoonful.

Blanched Almonds, 10.
Cinnamon, 1 teaspoonful.

Knead the butter and sugar into the dough. Roll into sticks the size of a finger and thirteen inches long. Chop the almonds and mix with sugar and cinnamon. Roll the sticks in this mixture till dusted all over with nuts and sugar, then shape into oblong rings, with one end crossing at the middle to the opposite side. Let them rise till nearly doubled, and bake.

PUDDINGS.

APRICOT PUDDING.

Rice, 1 scant cup.
Boiling water. 2 cups.
Butter, 1 tablespoonful..
Sugar, ½ cup.

Salt, 1 teaspoonful.
Egg, 1.
Apricots, ½ can.
Crumbs, ½ cup.

Wash the rice and cook in the double boiler one-half hour with the water, then add the butter, salt, sugar and egg well beaten. Butter generously a three-pint charlotte russe mould, sprinkle with crumbs. Put in a layer of rice one-half inch thick, and cover with apricots drained from the juice, and so continue till the mould is full. Cover with buttered crumbs and bake twenty minutes. Serve with apricot sauce. Almost any sort of fruit may be substituted for the apricots.

PRUNE RICE PUDDING.

Rice, ½ cup.
Boiling water, 3 pints.
Salt, ½ teaspoonful.

Sugar, 1 tablespoonful.
Prunes, ½ lb.

Wash the rice and add salt, sugar and water, bake one hour. Have the prunes cooked till soft, and stoned, and stir into the rice. Cook slowly two hours longer, or till the rice and prunes are cooked to a creamy consistency. Stir it often. Beat the whites of two eggs till stiff and dry and then beat in gradually two tablespoonfuls of powdered sugar, with a spoon. Press through a pastry bag and garnish the top. Brown in a very slow oven.

CREAM RICE PUDDING.

Rice, scant ½ cup,
Sugar, ¼ cup.

Milk, 3 pints.
Flavoring, 1 teaspoonful.

Wash the rice and mix in a pudding dish with milk, sugar and flavoring. Bake in a moderate oven three hours. Stir it often, adding the milk from time to time, if all can not be put in at first. The thinly shaved rind of an orange or lemon gives a pleasant flavor. The pudding should bake slowly and be creamy when done.

DELICATE PUDDING.

Water, 1¼ cup.
Fruit juice, 1 cup.
Corn starch, 3 tablespoonfuls.

Salt, ½ saltspoonful.
Sugar, ½ to 1½ cups.
Whites of eggs, 3.

Boil one cup of water and fruit juice, moisten the corn starch with the one-fourth cup of cold water, and add the boiling syrup. Cook five minutes, stirring all the time. Then add sugar and salt, and when dissolved, *fold* in the whites of the eggs beaten only till stiff and moist, *not dry.* Turn into a mould. Serve cold with boiled custard or fruit sauce.

Fresh or canned fruit may be used. All kinds are nice. Only one-half cup of lemon juice will be needed, fill the cup with water. Lemon will take one and a half cups of sugar. Canned fruits less than fresh.

Steamed Cabinet Pudding.

Eggs, 3.
Sugar, 3 tablespoonfuls.
Milk, 3 cups.

Fruit, 1 cup.
Stale cake, 3 pints.
Butter, 1 tablespoonful.

Use the butter to butter a three pint melon mould. The fruit may be currants, raisins and citrons mixed or candied, canned or fresh fruit. Sprinkle the mould with fruit and then break in the cake, or the mould may be lined with lady fingers, or macaroons. Beat the eggs, add sugar, salt and milk and pour over the cake. Let the pudding stand an hour and steam one and one-fourth hours. Serve with creamy sauce. Stale bread may be substituted for the cake.

Steamed Cottage Pudding.

Flour, 2 cups.
Milk, 1 cup.
Sugar, 1 cup.

Eggs, 2.
Melted Butter, 1 tablespoonful.
Baking Powder, 2 teaspoonfuls.
Nutmeg, one-fourth.

Cream the butter, add the sugar, then the eggs, and beat till very light, add the nutmeg and milk, and then the flour and baking powder, sifted together. Turn into a well buttered two quart mould. Steam one and one-fourth hours. Serve with a fruit sauce.

SNOW BALLS.

Eggs, 3.
Sugar, 1 cup.
Flour, 1 scant cup.
Lemon Juice, 2 tablespoonfuls.

Baking Powder, 1½ teaspoonfuls.
Water, 3 tablespoonfuls.
Grated yellow rind of 1 lemon.

Beat the yolks of eggs and sugar till very light. Add the water and rind and juice of the lemon. Beat the whites to a stiff dry froth. Turn these into the beaten mixture, and then sift in the flour and baking powder mixed together. *Fold* till well mixed. Turn into twelve or fifteen well buttered little earthen cups, and steam thirty minutes. When done roll the snow balls in powdered sugar and serve with strawberry sauce.

CREAM PUDDING.

Milk, 1 quart.
Eggs, 4.
Flour, 4 tablespoonfuls.

Salt ½ teaspoonful.
Sugar, 1 cup.
Fruit Juice, 4 tablespoonfuls.

Put three cups of milk into the double boiler. Beat the eggs; moisten the flour and salt with the one cup of cold milk, being careful to make the mixture smooth. Turn into the milk when scalded, and when it thickens add the eggs, and cook five minutes. Stir rapidly at first. Turn into a deep dish, and sprinkle the sugar over the top, pour upon it the fruit juice. Serve when perfectly cold.

CARAMEL RICE PUDDING.

Rice, 1 cup.
Milk, 1¼ quarts.
Salt, 1 teaspoonful.

Eggs, 2.
Cinnamon, 1 inch stick.
Sugar, ½ cup.

Wash the rice and soak in cold water for two hours, drain off the water and place in the double boiler with the milk and cinnamon and cook two hours.

Put the sugar in a small frying-pan and stir till it is brown and liquid. Pour this instantly into a plain warm mould, and turn the mould till the caramel coats all parts of it. Work rapidly for the sugar stiffens as soon as cold.

Now add the salt and the beaten egg to the rice and stir well. Turn the rice into the caramel lined mould, cover it, set it in a pan of hot water and bake thirty minutes. After removing from the oven let it stand on the table for ten minutes. Turn out onto a platter and serve with a cold boiled custard. Flavor the custard with vanilla or caramel.

CUSTARD SOUFFLÉ.

Butter, 2 tablespoonfuls, scant.
Flour, 2 tablespoonfuls.

Milk, 1 cup.
Eggs, 4.

Scald the milk in the double boiler, cream the butter, add the flour and pour the milk on gradually. Cook eight minutes, then add the yolks of the eggs well beaten, and set away to cool. When cold *fold* in the whites of the eggs beaten to a stiff dry froth. Turn into a slightly buttered pudding dish, and bake in a moderate oven thirty minutes. Serve at once with *creamy sauce.*

PUDDING SAUCES.

APRICOT OF FRUIT SAUCE.

Fruit Juice, 1 cup. Corn Starch, 1 teaspoonful.
Sugar, ½ cup. Cold Water, ½ cup.

Bring the sugar and fruit juice to a boil, moisten the corn starch with the cold water, add to the syrup and boil five minutes. Use any kind of fruit.

STRAWBERRY SAUCE.

Mash one quart of fresh strawberries and pour over them one cup of sugar. Let the fruit stand two hours. Just before serving time turn into a granite or porcelain-lined kettle, and bring to a boil, no more.

FRUIT SAUCE.

Put one pint of boiling water into a sauce pan. Moisten one tablespoonful of cornstarch with one-third cup of cold water and turn into the boiling water, boil ten minutes. Then add one pint of preserved fruit. If canned fruit is used boil one cup of sugar with the corn starch. If fresh fruit is used use a little more sugar.

The fruit may be left whole, or the sauce strained.

Lemon Sauce.

Moisten one tablespoonful of cornstarcn with one-fourth of a cup of cold water and pour into one cup of boiling water. Boil two minutes. Add the juice and grated rind of one lemon, and one cup of sugar.

Beat one egg very light. Pour the boiling sauce over it in a fine stream beating it with a spoon all the time.

Nutmeg Sauce.

Boil one cup of water, and add to it one tablespoonful of cornstarch, moistened with one cup of cold water, and when it boils add one cup of sugar, one fourth tablespoonful of salt, and one-third of a grated nutmeg. Boil slowly one-half hour, add two tablespoonfuls of butter and serve.

Egg Sauce.

Eggs, 3.　　　　　　　Extract, 1 teaspoonful.
Powdered sugar, 1 cup.

Beat the eggs separately, and when the whites

are very stiff and light *beat* in the sugar a little at a time, with a spoon. When very light, add the extract and the yolks of the eggs and continue to beat till very light. Serve at once.

CREAMY SAUCE.

Butter, ½ cup.
Powdered sugar, 1 cup.

Cream, ¼ cup.
Vanilla. 1 teaspoonful.

Cream the butter and then stir in the sugar a little at a time and beat till very light. Then add the cream and extract, a little at a time.

Just before serving, set the bowl into a pan of hot water, and as soon as the sauce is smooth and creamy, remove from the fire. It should not be heated enough to melt the sugar. Omit the cream and do not cook it, and you have a nice cold hard sauce for puddings.

CARAMEL SAUCE.

Put one-half cup of sugar in the frying pan and when melted and light brown add one-half cup of boiling water and boil slowly ten minutes.

DESSERTS.

ATALANTA APPLES.

Apples, 6.
Sugar, 1 pint.
Boiling water, 1 pint.

Cinnamon, one-inch stick.
Bread, 12 slices.
Jelly, ½ tumbler.

Boil the sugar, water and cinnamon ten minutes and skim. Core and halve the apples. Cook them in the syrup till tender, watching them carefully, turning them often. As soon as tender remove from the syrup on to plates, and cook in the top of the oven for five minutes. Cut rounds from the bread and dip them into the syrup and place on a platter. Nearly cover these with a thin layer of jelly. Place one piece of apple on each slice of bread. Boil the syrup remaining in the sauce pan till ropy, and then pour over the apples. Place a small piece of jelly on top of each apple. When cold garnish with whipped cream and bits of jelly.

APPLE SNOW.

Baked sour apples, 3.
Whites of eggs, 1.

Sugar. ½ cup.
Lemon juice, 2 tablespoonfuls.

Strain the pulp of the apples, add sugar and the white of egg beaten to a stiff, dry froth. Beat all with a wire spoon till stiff and white, add the lemon juice, pile in a glass dish and serve with boiled custard.

Boiled Custard.

Milk, 1 pint.
Yolks of eggs, 4.
Sugar, ½ cup.

Salt, ½ saltspoonful.
Flavoring, 1 teaspoonful.

Put 1½ cups of milk into the double boiler. Beat the egg and sugar till creamy, add one-half cup of cold milk, and turn into the milk when scalded. Cook till the custard stiffens and will coat the spoon. Strain into a bowl, and when cold add salt and flavoring.

For Caramel Custard.—Put the sugar into a frying pan and when melted and brown add two tablespoonfuls of water and pour into the milk in the double boiler, and proceed as for plain custard.

Fruit Tapioca.

Pearled Tapioca, ⅔ cup.
Boiling water, 1½ pints.
Sugar, ¼ cup.

Salt, 1 saltspoonful.
Currant jelly, ½ tumbler.

Wash the tapioca and put into the double boiler with the water, cook one hour, or till perfectly transparent, stirring often. Then add sugar, salt and jelly. Stir till well mixed and then turn into a mould and let it get very cold. Turn into a glass dish, and serve with sugar, and plain or whipped cream.

Or, use in place of the jelly, one-half cup of lemon juice, or any sort of acid fruit juice.

Or, one cup of canned fruit, like apricots, peaches, or quinces.

Or, one pint of ripe berries. Use more sugar as needed.

Or, a pleasing variety is to make the fruit tapioca and flavor with lemon juice. Color pink with cochineal coloring. Put alternate layers of tapioca, sliced bananas, and ripe strawberries, into a mould. Serve with whipped cream.

LEMON TAPIOCA.

Make like the fruit tapioca, adding one cup of sugar, and in place of the jelly, add grated rind and juice of one lemon and the yolks of two beaten eggs. Beat the whites of the eggs to a stiff, dry froth, and then beat in gradually, two tablespoonfuls of powdered sugar. Pile on top of the tapioca after it is put into the dish for serving, and brown slightly in a very slow oven. Let it get perfectly cold before serving.

Lemon Jelly.

Gelatine, ½ box.
Cold water, 1 scant cup.
Boiling water, 1 pint.

Sugar, 1 cup.
Lemon juice, ½ cup, generous.
Cinnamon, 1 inch stick.

Soak the gelatine in the cold water. Shave just the yellow rind of the lemon. Steep with the cinnamon in the boiling water ten minutes. Add the gelatine, sugar and lemon juice and when dissolved strain through a napkin.

Orange Charlotte.

Sour Orange pulp and juice, 1 cup.
Sweet oranges, 4.
Gelatine. ½ box.
Cold water, ½ cup.

Boiling water, 1 cup.
Sugar, 2 cups.
Whites of egg, 4 to 6.

Line a two quart Charlotte Russe mould with sections of sweet oranges. Keep the sections whole. Remove the seeds carefully and stand the sections on end in two rows around the sides of the mould.

Soak the gelatine in the cold water two hours, add the boiling water, and when dissolved add sugar, orange juice and pulp. Set the pan into another pan containing ice and water. When so stiff that it will drop from the spoon, beat the whites of the eggs to a stiff, dry froth, and beat into the orange mixture. Beat with a wire spoon till it is very light, smooth and stiff. Then turn into the mould lined with the sections of oranges.

Set it in the refrigerator for an hour or two. Serve with a boiled custard made with the yolks of the eggs.

CHARLOTTE RUSSE.

Gelatine, ½ box.
Cold water, ½ cup.
Cream, 1 quart.
Powdered sugar, ⅔ cup.

Vanilla, 2 teaspoonfuls.
Boiling water, ½ cup.
Lady fingers, two dozen.

Soak the gelatine in the cold water for two hours. Whip the cream and skim off the whip into a tin pan. Set this pan into a pan of ice water. When all the cream is whipped, drain off all the cream which has settled in the pan. Sprinkle the sugar over the whipped cream, and add the vanilla. Pour the boiling water on to the soaked gelatine, and when dissolved strain over the whipped cream. Stir rapidly but quietly, with the bowl of the spoon on the bottom of the pan. If the gelatine gets lumpy lift the pan from the water for a few moments, and if necessary, place it over a kettle of warm water for a moment till it becomes smooth again. When the gelatine in the bottom of the pan gets as stiff as a custard, fold in the cream on the top. Mix all gently, to keep the cream as light as possible. When so stiff it will only just pour, turn it into moulds lined with the lady fingers.

Line the mould by standing the lady fingers on end against the side, with the crust side next the mould. Leave a little space between the fingers. Strips of sponge cake may be used instead of the fingers.

ORANGE BAVARIAN CREAM.

Cream, 2 cups.
Oranges, 5.
Sugar, 1 cup.

Gelatine, ½ package.
Cold water, ½ cup.
Yolks of Eggs, 6.

Soak the gelatine in the cold water for two hours. Whip the cream till no more will whip. Skim the whip off into a pan, and put the unwhipped cream into the double boiler, Grate the rind of two oranges onto the gelatine. Squeeze the juice of the oranges. Beat the yolks of the eggs and the sugar till smooth and light, and add to the cream in the double boiler. When this thickens add the soaked gelatine, and when this is dissolved strain into a pan, set into a pan of ice water. Stir the orange juice into it, and continue to stir till as thick as a soft custard, then cut in the whipped cream. Do this quickly and gently, to keep the cream light.

When so stiff it will only just pour, turn into moulds.

PINEAPPLE BAVARIAN CREAM.

Pineapple, 1 can.
Sugar, 1 cup.
Cream, 1 pint.

Gelatine ½ box.
Cold water, ½ cup.
½ cup of boiling water.

Soak the gelatine in the cold water two hours.

Chop the pineapple or use the grated fruit. Cook the pineapple with the sugar ten minutes. Whip the cream, and skim off the froth into a pan. Dissolve the gelatine in the hot water, add to the pineapple and strain into a pan set in cold water. Mash through some of the fruit. Stir till as stiff as a thick custard, and then cut in the whipped cream. When so stiff it will only just pour, turn into molds.

Strawberry Bavarian Cream.

Make like the Pineapple, substituting one quart of mashed strawberries for the pineapple. Put the berries through a sieve fine enough to keep back the seeds. Use raspberries, peaches and apricots in the same way.

Directions for Freezing.

Pound or chip the ice, till the pieces are no bigger than walnuts. First put a layer of ice into the freezer about four inches deep, then put in a layer of salt, then a two inch layer of ice, and so continue till the ice and salt comes above the mixture in the can. Allow three pints of salt to a gallon of cream.

When the mixture is frozen, take out the dasher and pack the mixture down tightly. If the cream is to stand several hours, draw off the water and add more salt and ice.

DESSERTS.

ICE CREAM.

Milk, 1 pint.
Sugar, 2 cups.
Flour, 2 tablespoonfuls.
Salt, 1 saltspoonful.

Eggs, 2.
Cream, 1 quart.
Flavoring, 1 tablespoonful.

Scald the milk in the double boiler. Beat the eggs, flour and one cup of sugar together till light and then turn into the milk. Stir constantly till thickened and then occasionally. Cook in all twenty minutes. When cold add the second cup of sugar, the cream and flavoring, and strain into the freezer and freeze.

PHILADELPHIA ICE CREAM.

Cream, 1 quart.
Sugar, 1 cup.

Flavoring, 1 tablespoonful.

Scald the cream, and add the sugar. When cold add the flavoring and freeze. If the cream is very rich add 1 cup of milk. The whites of one or two eggs beaten till foamy may be used, in addition.

The following flavorings may be used with either of the preceding receipts as a foundation :

Chocolate Ice Cream :—

Scrape one ounce of Baker's chocolate, and cook till smooth and glossy with two tablespoonfuls of sugar and one of boiling water. Add this to the custard or cream while in the double boiler. When cold add $\frac{1}{2}$ tablespoonful of vanilla.

DESSERTS.

Macaroon Ice Cream :—

Dry, roll and sift macaroons to make one pint of crumbs. Omit one cup of the sugar given for the foundation. For *brown bread* ice cream, use brown bread crusts prepared in the same way.

Coffee Ice Cream:—

Use one cup of strong coffee, and measure the sugar generously.

Fruit Ice Cream:—

Use six bananas sifted, or one pint of strained strawberry or raspberry juice, or one pint of grated pineapple, or one pint of sifted peaches or apricots.

Caramel Ice Cream:—

Put one scant cup of sugar into a frying pan and stir over the fire till the sugar turns liquid and brown, add this to the hot custard, in place of one cup of the sugar.

ORANGE SHERBET.

Orange Juice, 1 pint.
Gelatine, 2 tablespoonfuls.
Cold Water, 3 cups.

Hot Water, 1 cup.
Sugar, 1 pint.
Lemons, 1.

Soak the gelatine in one-half cup of cold water. Dissolve in the boiling water, and add the remainder of the cold water, sugar and orange and lemon juice. Strain and freeze. For lemon sherbet use one cup of lemon juice.

STRAWBERRY SHERBET.

Preserved fruit, 1 pint.
Sugar, 1 cup.
Gelatine, 1 tablespoonful.

Water, 1 quart.
Lemons, 2.

Mash, and strain out the seeds, and proceed as for orange sherbet. Or, when fresh fruit is used make just the same as orange sherbet.

FROZEN APRICOTS.

Apricots, 1 can.
Water, 1 quart.

Sugar, 1 pint.
Whipped cream, 1 pint.

Mash up the apricots, and add sugar and water, and freeze. When nearly frozen, remove the dasher and mix in the whipped cream with a spoon, or use whites of three or four eggs beaten till frothy, and beat in just before the dasher is removed.

FRUIT SHERBET. (Prepared Quickly.)

Use one pint of any sort of fruit juice, made quite sweet with sugar, add *shaved ice* till stiff, and serve immediately. The "Gem" ice shave is the best for the purpose.

www.ingramcontent.com/pod-product-compliance
Lightning Source LLC
Chambersburg PA
CBHW031407160426
43196CB00007B/936